THE CANADIAN BAR ASSOCIATION

CODE OF PROFESSIONAL CONDUCT

ADOPTED BY COUNCIL, AUGUST 2004 AND FEBRUARY 2006

CODE OF PROFESSIONAL CONDUCT

ISBN 1-897086-28-8

Published by the Canadian Bar Association

The CBA gratefully acknowledges the generous financial support of the Canadian Bar Law for the Future Fund.

Ethics and Professional Issues Committee
Guylène Beaugé (2000-2004)
Kathryn A. Berge, Q.C. (2000-2002)
Louis Charette (2004-2006)
David C. Day, Q.C. (2004-2006)
Neil G. Gabrielson, Q.C. (2000-2002, 2004-2005)
Gregory D. Goulin, Q.C. (2000-2002)
Lois R. Hoegg, Q.C. (2000-2004)
Jacqueline L. King (2004-2006)
Peter Macdonald (2002-2004)
Priti Shah (2002-2004)
Alan J. Stern, Q.C. (2002-2006)

Counsel to the Committee
Gavin A. MacKenzie

Staff Liaison
Tamra L. Thomson, Director, Legislation and Law Reform
Richard Ellis, Legal Policy Analyst
Kerri Froc, Legal Policy Analyst

Production
CBA Communications

First printing 1974
Revised and adopted by Council, August 1987
Revised edition 1996
Revised edition 2006: amendments adopted by Council, August 2004 and February 2006

© Canadian Bar Association 2006
  Suite 500, 865 Carling Avenue
  Ottawa ON K1S 5S8
  info@cba.org
  Available online at www.cba.org

Principles of Civility for Advocates © The Advocates' Society. Reprinted with permission.

TABLE OF CONTENTS

Page

PRESIDENT'S MESSAGE

Standards of professional ethics form the backdrop for everything lawyers do. In adhering to codes of conduct, we uphold the long-standing values of our profession and ensure protection of the public. Some rules, such as the duty to act with integrity, will never change. Other rules must be revised from time to time to reflect changes in our society and in the way lawyers work.

In 2000, the CBA's Standing Committee on Ethics and Professional Issues was tasked with modernizing the model Code of Professional Conduct. The Committee undertook extensive research and several consultations with the profession, to identify issues and formulate recommendations. In August 2004 and in February 2006, CBA Council unanimously adopted the changes reflected herein.

The task could not be accomplished without the contributions of many people. On behalf of the CBA, I would like to express my gratitude to those who dedicated time and expertise to the project:

- Committee members Guylène Beaugé, Kathryn A. Berge, Q.C., Louis Charette, David C. Day, Q.C., Neil G. Gabrielson, Q.C., Gregory D. Goulin, Q.C., Lois R. Hoegg, Q.C., Jacqueline L. King , Peter Macdonald, Priti Shah and Alan J. Stern, Q.C.

- Counsel to the Committee, Gavin A. MacKenzie of Heenan Blaikie LLP.

- Editors Elizabeth F. Judge (English) and Patrice Deslauriers (French) and their assistants.

- Tamra L. Thomson, Richard Ellis and Kerri A. Froc, staff lawyers who steered the project from the CBA Legal and Governmental Affairs Department.

- Joanna Fine, who updated the footnote references to the Codes of Conduct of Canadian jurisdictions and the ABA Model Code and Model Rules.

- C. Paul Daniels, a retired member of the Law Society of British Columbia, who devoted a good deal of time and effort to improving the drafting of the proposed revisions.

- The many members and organizations who, throughout the project, made thoughtful and constructive submissions on possible revisions to the Code.

The CBA could not have undertaken this project without generous financial assistance from the Canadian Bar Law for the Future Fund. Since its inception, the LFFF has helped finance more than 100 projects that will help shape a better future for lawyers and the law. I encourage you to make a contribution today.

The CBA is justifiably proud of the Code of Professional Conduct, as a contribution to the delivery of competent legal services according to the highest ethical traditions of our profession.

Brian A. Tabor, Q.C.
President
Ottawa, March 2006

PREFACE [1]

The legal profession has developed over the centuries to meet a public need for legal services on a professional basis. Traditionally, this has involved the provision of advice and representation to protect or advance the rights, liberties and property of a client by a trusted adviser with whom the client has a personal relationship and whose integrity, competence and loyalty are assured.[2]

In order to satisfy this need for legal services adequately, lawyers and the quality of service they provide must command the confidence and respect of the public. This can only be achieved if lawyers establish and maintain a reputation for both integrity and high standards of legal skill and care. The lawyers of many countries in the world, despite differences in their legal systems, practices, procedures and customs, have all imposed upon themselves substantially the same basic standards. Those standards invariably place their main emphasis on integrity and competence.

In Canada, the provincial legislatures have entrusted to the legal profession through its governing bodies responsibility for maintaining standards of professional conduct and for disciplining lawyers who fail to meet them. Generally, the preparation and publication of codes of ethics and professional conduct have been left to the profession. It is a responsibility that must be accepted and carried out by the profession as a whole.

The pertinent laws in Canada use various terms to describe conduct that subjects the lawyer to discipline, for example, "professional misconduct", "conduct unbecoming" and "acts derogatory to the honour or dignity of the Bar". Some statutes also provide that disciplinary action may be taken if a lawyer is convicted of an indictable offence or for "misappropriation or wrongful conversion" or "gross negligence" or for conduct "incompatible with the best interests of the public or the members of the [Law] Society" or for breach of the applicable statute itself or the rules made under it.[3]

With few exceptions the statutes do not specify the kinds of conduct that will subject a lawyer to discipline. For its part, the Code does not attempt to define professional misconduct or conduct unbecoming; nor does it try to evaluate the relative importance of the various rules or the gravity of a breach of any of them. Those functions are the responsibility of the various governing bodies. The rules that follow are therefore intended to serve as a guide, and the commentaries and notes appended to them are illustrative only. By enunciating principles of what is and is not acceptable professional conduct, the Code is designed to assist governing bodies and practitioners alike in determining whether in a given case the conduct is acceptable, thus furthering the process of self-government.

The essence of professional responsibility is that the lawyer must act at all times *uberrimae fidei*, with utmost good faith to the court, to the client, to other lawyers, and to members of the public. Given the many and varied demands to which the lawyer is subject, it is inevitable that problems will arise. No set of rules can foresee every possible situation, but the ethical principles set out in the Code are intended to provide a framework within which the lawyer may, with courage and dignity, provide the high quality of legal services that a complex and ever-changing society demands.[4]

The extent to which each lawyer's conduct should rise above the minimum standards set by the Code is a matter of personal decision. The lawyer who would enjoy the respect and confidence of the community as well as of other members of the legal profession must strive to maintain the highest possible degree of ethical conduct. The greatness and strength of the legal profession depend on high standards of professional conduct that permit no compromise.

The Code of Professional Conduct that follows is to be understood and applied in the light of its primary concern for the protection of the public interest. This principle is implicit in the legislative grants of self-government referred to above. Inevitably, the practical application of the Code to the diverse situations that confront an active profession in a changing society will reveal gaps, ambiguities and apparent inconsistencies.[5] In such cases, the principle of protection of the public interest will serve to guide the practitioner to the applicable principles of ethical conduct and the true intent of the Code.

---

[1]The footnotes relate the provisions of the Code to pertinent earlier Codes, rulings, by-laws, statutes, judicial dicta, text books and articles, as well as to certain other materials They are selective, not exhaustive, and merely supplement the text. For abbreviations and bibliography, see pp. 143 and 145.

[2]"The core of the proposition is that problems of...rights or property call for a personal relationship with a trusted adviser, whose discretion is absolute, who serves no master but his client, and whose competence is assured. The codes and traditions of the professions who supply these services support the basic proposition. They also display the uniformity that its truth would lead one to expect." *Bennion*, p. 16.

[3] Abstract of disciplinary provisions:

Alberta: *Legal Profession Act*, R.S.A. 2000, c. L-8.

    s. 49   "conduct ... incompatible with the best interests of the public or of the members of the Society"

            "tends to harm the standing of the legal profession generally"

British Columbia: *Legal Profession Act*, S.B.C. 1998, c. 9.

    s. 38   "professional misconduct"

            "conduct unbecoming a lawyer"

            "breach of this Act or the rules"

    s. 36   "convicted of an offence that may only be prosecuted on indictment"

Manitoba: *Legal Profession Act*, C.C.S.M., c. L-107.

    s. 63   "professional misconduct"

            "conduct unbecoming a lawyer or student"

New Brunswick: *Law Society Act*, 1996, S.N.B. 1996, c. 89.

    s. 38   "professional misconduct"

            "conduct unbecoming a member of the Society"

            "acting in breach of this Act or the rules"

Newfoundland: *Law Society Act*, 1999, S.N.L. 1999, c. L-9.1.

    s. 41   "professional misconduct"

            "conduct unbecoming a member of the Society"

"acting in breach of this Act or the rules"
"failing to adhere to the Code of Professional Conduct"
Nova Scotia: *Legal Profession Act*, S.N.S. 2004, c. 28.
s. 33 "professional misconduct"
"conduct unbecoming a lawyer"
Ontario: *Law Society Act*, R.S.O. 1990, c.L-8, as am.
s. 33 "professional misconduct"
"conduct unbecoming a barrister or solicitor"
"conduct unbecoming a student member"
Prince Edward Island: *Legal Profession Act*, R.S.P.E.I. 1988, c. L-6.1.
s. 37 "conduct unbecoming a member or professional misconduct"
"conduct...contrary to the best interests of the public or of the legal profession"
"likely to harm the standing of the legal profession"
"contrary to any code or standard of ethics adopted by the society"
"misconduct by, or conduct unbecoming, an articled clerk"
Quebec: *An Act respecting the Barreau du Québec*, R.S.Q., c. B-1.
s. 122 "position or an office...incompatible with the practice or dignity of the profession of advocate"
Saskatchewan: *Legal Profession Act*, 1990, S.S. 1990-91, c. L-10.1, as am.
ss. 2 and 40 "conduct unbecoming"
England: *Cordery on Solicitors* (7th ed., 1981), p. 333.
"...because he has been guilty of an act or omission for which the Act or some other statute prescribes that penalty, or because he has committed an act of misconduct which renders him unfit to be permitted to continue in practice."
(at p. 335): "Misconduct which makes a solicitor unfit to continue in practice may be divided into three kinds: criminal conduct, professional misconduct and unprofessional conduct."
(at p. 336): "The jurisdiction is not limited to cases where the misconduct charged amounts to an indictable offence, or is professional in character, but extends to all cases where the solicitor's conduct is 'unprofessional', i.e., such as renders him unfit to be an officer of the court."
"Is it a personally disgraceful offence or is it not? Ought any respectable solicitor to be called upon to enter into that intimate discourse with [the offender] which is necessary between two solicitors even though they are acting for opposite parties?" per Lord Esher M.R. in *Re Weare* (1893), 2 Q.B. 439 at 446 (C.A.).
"Counsel...takes the position that the expressions [unprofessional conduct and professional misconduct] are synonymous. I agree...that the phrases are often used interchangeably but cannot agree that this is always so... Accepting as I do that the terms are not synonymous..." per McKay J. in *Re Novak and Law Society* (1973) 31 D.L.R. (3d) 89 at 102 (B.C.S.C.).
4 "The law and its institutions change as social conditions change. They must change if they are to preserve, much less advance, the political and social values from which they derive their purposes and their life. This is true of the most important of legal

institutions, the profession of law. The profession, too, must change when conditions change in order to preserve and advance the social values that are its reason for being." Cheatham, *Availability of Legal Services: The Responsibility of the Individual Lawyer and the Organized Bar* (1965) 12 U.C.L.A. L. Rev. 438, 440.

[5] "It is not possible to frame a set of rules which will particularize all the duties of the lawyer in all the varied relations of his professional life...", Sask. *Preamble*.

INTERPRETATION

In this Code the field of professional conduct and ethics is divided into twenty-two chapters, each of which contains a short statement of a rule or principle followed by commentary and notes. Although this division gives rise to some overlapping of subjects, the principle of integrity enunciated in Chapter I underlies the entire Code, so that some of the rules in subsequent chapters represent particular applications of the basic rule set out in Chapter I. Again there are instances where substantially the same comment appears more than once. Such duplication is desirable to provide clarity and emphasis and to reduce cross-references.

The commentary and notes to each rule discuss the ethical considerations involved, explanations, examples, and other material designed to assist in the interpretation and understanding of the rule itself. Each rule should therefore be read with and interpreted in the light of the related commentary and notes.

Certain terms used in the Code require definition:

"client"   means a person on whose behalf a lawyer renders or undertakes to render professional services;

"court"   includes conventional law courts and generally all judicial and quasi-judicial tribunals;

"Governing Body"   means the body charged under the laws of a particular jurisdiction with the duty of governing the legal profession (e.g., the Benchers, General Council, Convocation or Council);

"lawyer"	means an individual who is duly authorized to practise law;
"legal profession"	refers to lawyers collectively;
"person"	includes a corporation or other legal entity, an association, partnership or other organization, the Crown in right of Canada or a province or territory and the government of a state or any political subdivision thereof.

The term "lawyer" as defined above extends not only to those engaged in private practice but also to those who are employed by governments, agencies, corporations and other organizations. An employer-employee relationship of this kind may give rise to special problems in the area of conflict of interest,[1] but in all matters involving integrity[2] and generally in all professional matters, if the requirements or demands of the employer conflict with the standards declared by the Code, the latter must govern.

---

[1] See Chapter V.

[2] See Chapter I. The involvement of various lawyers in the Watergate affair most graphically illustrates some of the hazards.

CHAPTER I

INTEGRITY

RULE

The lawyer must discharge with integrity all duties owed to clients, the court or tribunal or other members of the profession and the public.[1]

Commentary

Guiding Principles

1.   Integrity is the fundamental quality of any person who seeks to practise as a member of the legal profession. If the client is in any doubt about the lawyer's trustworthiness, the essential element in the lawyer-client relationship will be missing. If personal integrity is lacking the lawyer's usefulness to the client and reputation within the profession will be destroyed regardless of how competent the lawyer may be.[2]

2.   The principle of integrity is a key element of each rule of the Code.[3]

Disciplinary Action

3.   Dishonourable or questionable conduct on the part of the lawyer in either private life or professional practice will reflect adversely upon the lawyer, the integrity of the legal profession

and the administration of justice as a whole. If the conduct, whether within or outside the professional sphere, is such that knowledge of it would be likely to impair the client's trust in the lawyer as a professional consultant, a governing body may be justified in taking disciplinary action.[4]

Non-Professional Activities

4.   Generally speaking, however, a governing body will not be concerned with the purely private or extra-professional activities of a lawyer that do not bring into question the integrity of the legal profession or the lawyer's professional integrity or competence.

5.   Illustrations of conduct that may infringe the Rule (and often other provisions of this Code) include:

    (a) committing any personally disgraceful or morally reprehensible offence that reflects upon the lawyer's integrity (of which a conviction by a competent court would be *prima facie* evidence);

    (b) committing, whether professionally or in the lawyer's personal capacity, any act of fraud or dishonesty, e.g., by knowingly making a false tax return or falsifying a document, whether or not prosecuted for so doing;

    (c) making an untrue representation or concealing a material fact from a client, with a dishonest or improper motive;

    (d) taking advantage of the youth, inexperience, lack of education or sophistication, ill health, or unbusinesslike habits of a client;

    (e) misappropriating or dealing dishonestly with a client's money or other property;

    (f) receiving money or other property from or on behalf of a client for a specific purpose and failing, without the client's consent, to pay or apply it for that purpose;

(g) knowingly assisting, enabling or permitting any person to act fraudulently, dishonestly or illegally;
(h) failing to be absolutely frank and candid in all dealings with the Court or tribunal, fellow lawyers, and other parties to proceedings, subject always to not betraying the client's cause, abandoning the client's legal rights or disclosing the client's confidences; and
(i) failing to honour the lawyer's word when pledged even though, under technical rules, the absence of writing might afford a legal defence.

---

[1] ABA-MC Canon 1; B.C. 2; N.B. 1-R, 1-C.1; Ont. 6.01(1); N.S. 1-R; Que. 2.00.01, 3.02.01. *Oxford English Dictionary* (2d ed.) *s.v.* "integrity": "Soundness of moral principle; the character of uncorrupted virtue, esp. in relation to truth and fair dealing; uprightness, honesty, sincerity."
[2] Ont. 6.01(1) Commentary; N.S. 1.1.
[3] N.B. 1-C.2.
[4] ABA-MC DR 1-101; N.B. 1-C.3; N.S. 1.2.

CHAPTER II

COMPETENCE AND QUALITY OF SERVICE

RULE

1. The lawyer owes the client a duty to be competent to perform any legal services undertaken on the client's behalf.[1]

2. The lawyer should serve the client in a conscientious, diligent and efficient manner so as to provide a quality of service at least equal to that which lawyers generally would expect of a competent lawyer in a like situation.[2]

Commentary

Knowledge and Skill

1. Competence in the context of the first branch of this Rule goes beyond formal qualification to practise law. It has to do with the sufficiency of the lawyer's qualifications to deal with the matter in question. It includes knowledge, skill, and the ability to use them effectively in the interests of the client.[3]

2. As members of the legal profession, lawyers hold themselves out as being knowledgeable, skilled and capable in the practice of law. The client is entitled to assume that the lawyer has the ability and capacity to deal adequately with any legal matters undertaken on the client's behalf.[4]

3.   The lawyer should not undertake a matter without honestly feeling either competent to handle it, or able to become competent without undue delay, risk or expense to the client. The lawyer who proceeds on any other basis is not being honest with the client. This is an ethical consideration and is to be distinguished from the standard of care that a court would apply for purposes of determining negligence.[5]

4.   Competence involves more than an understanding of legal principles; it involves an adequate knowledge of the practice and procedures by which those principles can be effectively applied. To accomplish this, the lawyer should keep abreast of developments in all areas in which the lawyer practises. The lawyer should also develop and maintain a facility with advances in technology in areas in which the lawyer practises to maintain a level of competence that meets the standard reasonably expected of lawyers in similar practice circumstances.[6]

5.   In deciding whether the lawyer has employed the requisite degree of knowledge and skill in a particular matter, relevant factors will include the complexity and specialized nature of the matter, the lawyer's general experience, the lawyer's training and experience in the field in question, the preparation and study the lawyer is able to give the matter and whether it is appropriate or feasible to refer the matter to, or associate or consult with, a lawyer of established competence in the field in question. In some circumstances expertise in a particular field of law may be required; often the necessary degree of proficiency will be that of the general practitioner.[7]

Seeking Assistance

6.   The lawyer must be alert to recognize any lack of competence for a particular task and the disservice that would be done the client by undertaking that task. If consulted in

such circumstances, the lawyer should either decline to act or obtain the client's instructions to retain, consult or collaborate with a lawyer who is competent in that field. The lawyer should also recognize that competence for a particular task may sometimes require seeking advice from or collaborating with experts in scientific, accounting or other non-legal fields. In such a situation the lawyer should not hesitate to seek the client's instructions to consult experts.[8]

Quality of Service

7. Numerous examples could be given of conduct that does not meet the quality of service required by the second branch of the Rule. The list that follows is illustrative, but not by any means exhaustive:

    (a) failure to keep the client reasonably informed;

    (b) failure to answer reasonable requests from the client for information;

    (c) unexplained failure to respond to the client's telephone calls;

    (d) failure to keep appointments with clients without explanation or apology;

    (e) informing the client that something will happen or that some step will be taken by a certain date, then letting the date pass without follow-up information or explanation;

    (f) failure to answer within a reasonable time a communication that requires a reply;

    (g) doing the work in hand but doing it so belatedly that its value to the client is diminished or lost;

    (h) slipshod work, such as mistakes or omissions in statements or documents prepared on behalf of the client;

    (i) failure to maintain office staff and facilities adequate to the lawyer's practice;

(j)   failure to inform the client of proposals of settlement, or to explain them properly;

(k)   withholding information from the client or misleading the client about the position of a matter in order to cover up the fact of neglect or mistakes;

(l)   failure to make a prompt and complete report when the work is finished or, if a final report cannot be made, failure to make an interim report where one might reasonably be expected;

(m) self-induced disability, for example from the use of intoxicants or drugs, which interferes with or prejudices the lawyer's services to the client.

Promptness

8.   The requirement of conscientious, diligent and efficient service means that the lawyer must make every effort to provide prompt service to the client. If the lawyer can reasonably foresee undue delay in providing advice or services, the client should be so informed.[9]

Consequences of Incompetence

9.   It will be observed that the Rule does not prescribe a standard of perfection. A mistake, even though it might be actionable for damages in negligence, would not necessarily constitute a failure to maintain the standard set by the Rule, but evidence of gross neglect in a particular matter or a pattern of neglect or mistakes in different matters may be evidence of such a failure regardless of tort liability. Where both negligence and incompetence are established, while damages may be awarded for the former, the latter can give rise to the additional sanction of disciplinary action.[10]

10. The lawyer who is incompetent does the client a disservice, brings discredit to the profession, and may bring

the administration of justice into disrepute. As well as damaging the lawyer's own reputation and practice, incompetence may also injure the lawyer's associates or dependants.[11]

---

[1] Alta. 2 S.O.P.; ABA-MC Canon 6; ABA-MR 1.1; B.C. 3(1); N.B. 2-R; Ont. 2.01(1), 2.01(2); N.S. 2-R.

[2] B.C.3(3); N.B. 3-R, 3-C.1; N.S. 3-R.

[3] N.S. 2.

[4] N.B. 2-C.2; N.S. 2.1; Ont. 2.01(1) Commentary; Que. 3.01.01, 3.02.03.

[5] Alta. 2-R.2; ABA-MC EC6-3, DR6-101A; N.B. 2-C.3; N.S. 2.3; Ont. 2.01(1) Commentary.

[6] ABA-MC EC 6-2; ABA-MR 1.1 [6]; N.B. 2-C.4; N.S. 2, 2.3.

[7] N.S. 2.5, 2.6.

[8] B.C. 3(4); N.B. 2-C.6, 2-C.7; N.S. 2.7, 2.8; Ont. 2.01(1) Commentary; Que. 3.01.01 and 3.01.02.

[9] B.C. 3(3); N.B. 3-C.4; N.S. 3.1.

[10] B.C. 3(5); N.B. 3-C.2.

[11] N.B. 2-C.8; N.S. 2.9, 3.2, 3.3; Ont. 2.01(2) Commentary.

[12] N.B. 2-C.9; N.S. 2.10; Ont. 2.01(1).

CHAPTER III

ADVISING CLIENTS

RULE

The lawyer must be both honest and candid when advising clients.[1]

Commentary

Scope of Advice

1. The lawyer's duty to the client who seeks legal advice is to give the client a competent opinion based on sufficient knowledge of the relevant facts, an adequate consideration of the applicable law and the lawyer's own experience and expertise. The advice must be open and undisguised, clearly disclosing what the lawyer honestly thinks about the merits and probable results.[2]

2. Whenever it becomes apparent that the client has misunderstood or misconceived what is really involved, the lawyer should explain as well as advise, so that the client is informed of the true position and fairly advised about the real issues or questions involved.[3]

3. The lawyer should clearly indicate the facts, circumstances and assumptions upon which the lawyer's opinion is based, particularly where the circumstances do not justify an

exhaustive investigation with resultant expense to the client. However, unless the client instructs otherwise, the lawyer should investigate the matter in sufficient detail to be able to express an opinion rather than merely make comments with many qualifications.[4]

4.   The lawyer should be wary of bold and confident assurances to the client, especially when the lawyer's employment may depend upon advising in a particular way.[5]

Second Opinion

5.   If the client so desires, the lawyer should assist in obtaining a second opinion.[6]

Compromise or Settlement

6.   The lawyer should advise and encourage the client to compromise or settle a dispute whenever possible on a reasonable basis and should discourage the client from commencing or continuing useless legal proceedings.[7]

Dishonesty or Fraud by Client

7.   When advising the client the lawyer must never knowingly assist in or encourage any dishonesty, fraud, crime or illegal conduct, or instruct the client on how to violate the law and avoid punishment. The lawyer should be on guard against becoming the tool or dupe of an unscrupulous client or of persons associated with such a client.[8]

Test Cases

8.   A *bona fide* test case is not necessarily precluded by the preceding paragraph and, so long as no injury to the person or violence is involved, the lawyer may properly advise and

represent a client who, in good faith and on reasonable grounds, desires to challenge or test a law, and this can most effectively be done by means of a technical breach giving rise to a test case. In all such situations the lawyer should ensure that the client appreciates the consequences of bringing a test case.[9]

Threatening Criminal or Disciplinary Proceedings

9. Apart from the substantive law on the subject, it is improper for the lawyer to advise, threaten or bring a criminal, quasi-criminal or disciplinary proceeding in order to secure some civil advantage for the client, or to advise, seek or procure the withdrawal of such a proceeding in consideration of the payment of money, or transfer of property, to or for the benefit of the client.[10]

Advice on Non-Legal Matters

10. In addition to opinions on legal questions, the lawyer may be asked for or expected to give advice on non-legal matters such as the business, policy or social implications involved in a question, or the course the client should choose. In many instances the lawyer's experience will be such that the lawyer's views on non-legal matters will be of real benefit to the client. The lawyer who advises on such matters should, where and to the extent necessary, point out the lawyer's lack of experience or other qualification in the particular field and should clearly distinguish legal advice from such other advice.[11]

Errors and Omissions

11. The duty to give honest and candid advice requires the lawyer to inform the client promptly of the facts, but without admitting liability, upon discovering that an error or omission has occurred in a matter for which the lawyer was engaged

and that is or may be damaging to the client and cannot readily be rectified. When so informing the client the lawyer should be careful not to prejudice any rights of indemnity that either of them may have under any insurance, client's protection or indemnity plan, or otherwise. At the same time the lawyer should recommend that the client obtain legal advice elsewhere about any rights the client may have arising from such error or omission and whether it is appropriate for the lawyer to continue to act in the matter. The lawyer should also give prompt notice of any potential claim to the lawyer's insurer and any other indemnitor so that any protection from that source will not be prejudiced and, unless the client objects, should assist and cooperate with the insurer or other indemnitor to the extent necessary to enable any claim that is made to be dealt with promptly. If the lawyer is not so indemnified, or to the extent that the indemnity may not fully cover the claim, the lawyer should expeditiously deal with any claim that may be made and must not, under any circumstances, take unfair advantage that might defeat or impair the client's claim. In cases where liability is clear and the insurer or other indemnitor is prepared to pay its portion of the claim, the lawyer is under a duty to arrange for payment of the balance.[12]

Giving Independent Advice

12. Where the lawyer is asked to provide independent advice or independent representation to another lawyer's client in a situation where a conflict exists, the provision of such advice or representation is an undertaking to be taken seriously and not lightly assumed or perfunctorily discharged. It involves a duty to the client for whom the independent advice or representation is provided that is the same as in any other lawyer and client relationship and ordinarily extends to the nature and result of the transaction.[13]

[1] Alta 9-S.0.P; B.C. 1(3); N.B. 4-R; N.S. 4; Ont. 2.02(1); Que. 3.01.01; M.M. Orkin, *Legal Ethics: A Study of Professional Conduct* (Toronto: Cartwright & Jane, 1957) at pp. 78-79.

[2] N.B. 4-C.1; Ont. 2.02(1) Commentary; N.S. 4 Guiding Principle. The lawyer should not remain silent when it is plain that the client is rushing into an "unwise, not to say disastrous adventure," per Lord Danckwerts in *Neushal v. Mellish & Harkavy* (1967), 111 Sol. Jo. 399 (C.A.).

[3] Alta. 9-R.12; N.B. 4-C.3; N.S. 4.1; Ont. 2.01(1) Commentary.

[4] N.S. 4.2, 4.3; Ont. 2.01(1) Commentary.

[5] N.B. 4-C.4; N.S. 4.4; Ont. 2.01(1) Commentary.

[6] Alta. 9-R.17; N.B. 4-C.5; N.S. 4.5.

[7] Alta. 9-R.16; N.B. 4-C.6; N.S. 4.6; Ont. 2.02(2); Que. 3.02.10.

[8] Alta. 9-R.11; N.B. 4-C.7; N.S. 4.7, 4.8; Ont. 2.02(5). Cf. ABA ECs 7-3 and 7-5: "Where the bounds of law are uncertain...the two roles [of advocate and adviser] are essentially different. In asserting a position on behalf of his client, an *advocate* for the most part *deals with past conduct* and must take the facts as he finds them. By contrast, a lawyer serving as *adviser* primarily *assists* his client *in determining* the course of future *conduct* and relationships.... A lawyer should never encourage or aid his client to commit criminal acts or counsel his client on how to violate the law and avoid punishment..." [emphasis added].

[9] N.S. 4.9; Ont. 2.02(5) Commentary. For example, to challenge the jurisdiction for or the applicability of a shop-closing by-law or a licensing measure, or to determine the rights of a class or group having some common interest.

[10] B.C. 4(2); N.B. 4-C.9; N.S. 4.10; Ont. 2.02(4). See "Criminal Law May Not be Used to Collect Civil Debts" (1968) 2:4 L. Soc'y Gaz. 36.

[11] N.B. 4-C.14; N.S. 4.11-4.13; Ont. 2.01(1) Commentary.

[12] Alta. 9-R.18; B.C. 4(5), 4(5.1); N.B. 4-C.16; N.S. 4.14-4.17.

[13] N.B. 4-C.13; N.S. 4.18, 4.19.

CHAPTER IV

CONFIDENTIAL INFORMATION

RULE

Maintaining Information in Confidence

1.   The lawyer has a duty to hold in strict confidence all information concerning the business and affairs of the client acquired in the course of the professional relationship, and shall not divulge any such information except as expressly or impliedly authorized by the client, required by law or otherwise required by this Code.[1]

Public Safety Exception

2.   Where a lawyer believes upon reasonable grounds that there is an imminent risk to an identifiable person or group of death or serious bodily harm, including serious psychological harm that would substantially interfere with health or well-being, the lawyer shall disclose confidential information where it is necessary to do so in order to prevent the death or harm, but shall not disclose more information than is required.[2]

3.   The lawyer who has reasonable grounds for believing that a dangerous situation is likely to develop at a court or tribunal facility shall inform the person having responsibility for security at the facility and give particulars, being careful not to disclose confidential information except as required by

paragraph 2 of this Rule. Where possible the lawyer should suggest solutions to the anticipated problem such as:

(a) the need for further security;
(b) that judgment be reserved;
(c) such other measure as may seem advisable.[3]

Disclosure Where Lawyer's Conduct in Issue

4. Disclosure may also be justified in order to establish or collect a fee, or to defend the lawyer or the lawyer's associates or employees against any allegation of malpractice or misconduct, but only to the extent necessary for such purposes.[4]

Commentary

Guiding Principles

1. The lawyer cannot render effective professional service to the client unless there is full and unreserved communication between them. At the same time the client must feel completely secure and entitled to proceed on the basis that, without an express request or stipulation on the client's part, matters disclosed to or discussed with the lawyer will be held secret and confidential.[5]

2. This ethical rule must be distinguished from the evidentiary rule of solicitor-client privilege with respect to oral or written communications passing between the client and the lawyer. The ethical rule is wider and applies without regard to the nature or source of the information or to the fact that others may share the knowledge.[6]

3. The importance of the even broader ethical rule regarding confidential information is illustrated by the Supreme Court

of Canada's approach to solicitor-client privilege. The Court has held that solicitor-client privilege must remain as close to absolute as possible if it is to retain its relevance. Solicitor-client privilege is a rule of evidence, an important civil and legal right and a principle of fundamental justice in Canadian law. The public has a compelling interest in maintaining the integrity of the solicitor-client relationship. Confidential communications to a lawyer represent an important exercise of the right to privacy, and they are central to the administration of justice in an adversarial system.

4. As a general rule, the lawyer should not disclose having been consulted or retained by a person except to the extent that the nature of the matter requires such disclosure.[7]

5 The lawyer owes a duty of secrecy to every client without exception, regardless of whether it is a continuing or casual client. The duty survives the professional relationship and continues indefinitely after the lawyer has ceased to act for the client, whether or not differences have arisen between them.[8]

6. The lawyer should take care to avoid disclosure to one client of confidential information concerning or received from another client and should decline employment that might require such disclosure.[9]

7. The lawyer should avoid indiscreet conversations, even with the lawyer's spouse or family, about a client's business or affairs and should shun gossip about such things even though the client is not named or otherwise identified. Likewise the lawyer should not repeat any gossip or information about the client's business or affairs that may be overheard by or recounted to the lawyer. Apart altogether from ethical considerations or questions of good taste, indiscreet shop-talk between lawyers, if overheard by third parties able to identify the matter being discussed, could result in prejudice to the

client. Moreover, the respect of the listener for the lawyers concerned and the legal profession generally will probably be lessened.[10]

8. Although the Rule may not apply to facts that are public knowledge, the lawyer should guard against participating in or commenting upon speculation concerning the client's affairs or business.[11]

Disclosure Authorized by Client

9. Confidential information may be divulged with the express authority of the client and, in some situations, that authority may be implied. For example, some disclosure may be necessary in a pleading or other document delivered in litigation being conducted for the client. Again, the lawyer may (unless the client directs otherwise) disclose the client's affairs to partners and associates in the firm and, to the extent necessary, to non-legal staff such as secretaries and filing clerks. This authority to disclose, whether express or implied, places on the lawyer a duty to impress upon partners, associates, students and employees the importance of non-disclosure (both during their employment and afterwards) and requires the lawyer to take reasonable care to prevent their disclosing or using information that the lawyer is bound to keep in confidence.[12]

Confidential Information Not to be Used

10. The fiduciary relationship between lawyer and client forbids the lawyer to use any confidential information covered by the ethical rule for the benefit of the lawyer or a third person, or to the disadvantage of the client. The lawyer who engages in literary work, such as an autobiography, should avoid disclosure of confidential information.[13]

Disclosure Required by Law

11. When disclosure is required by law or by order of a court of competent jurisdiction, the lawyer should be careful not to divulge more than is required. Legislation in certain jurisdictions imposes a duty on persons to report sexual or physical abuse in specified circumstances. Careful consideration of the wording of such legislation is necessary to determine whether, in such circumstances, communications that are subject to solicitor-client privilege must be disclosed.[14]

Whistleblowing

12. A lawyer employed or retained to act for an organization, including a corporation, confronts a difficult problem about confidentiality when the lawyer becomes aware that the organization may commit a dishonest, fraudulent, criminal, or illegal act. This problem is sometimes described as the problem of whether the lawyer should "blow the whistle" on the employer or client. Although this Code makes it clear that the lawyer shall not knowingly assist or encourage any dishonesty, fraud, crime, or illegal conduct (Chapter III, commentary 7), it does not follow that the lawyer should disclose to the appropriate authorities an employer's or client's proposed misconduct. Rather, the general rule, as set out above, is that the lawyer shall hold the client's information in strict confidence, and this general rule is subject to only a few exceptions. If the exceptions do not apply there are, however, several steps that a lawyer should take when confronted with this problem of proposed misconduct by an organization. The lawyer should recognize that the lawyer's duties are owed to the organization and not to its officers, employees, or agents. The lawyer should therefore ask that the matter be reconsidered, and should, if necessary, bring the proposed misconduct to the attention of a higher (and ultimately the highest) authority in the organization despite any direction

from anyone in the organization to the contrary. If these
measures fail, then it may be appropriate for the lawyer to
resign in accordance with the rules for withdrawal from
representation (Chapter XII).[15]

---

[1] Alta. 7-S.O.P., 7-R.1; ABA-MC Canon 4, DRs 4-101(A), (B), (C); ABA-MR 1.6(a);
B.C. 5(1); N.B. 5-R; N.S. 5; Ont. 2.03(1); Que. 3.06.01, 3.06.02.

[2] Alta. 7-R.8(c); ABA-MC DR4-101(c)(3); ABA-MR 1.6(b); B.C. 5(12); N.B. 5-
C.8(b); N.S. 5.12; Ont. 2.03(3); Que. 3.06.01.

[3] N.B. 5-C.11; Ont. 2.03(1) Commentary.

[4] Alta. 7-R.8 (e.1); ABA-MC DR4-101(c)(4); N.S. 5.11; Ont. 2.03(5).

[5] N.S. 5; Ont. 2.03(1) Commentary. "[I]t is absolutely necessary that a man, in order
to prosecute his rights or defend himself...should have recourse to lawyers
and...equally necessary...that he should be able to place unrestricted and unbounded
confidence in the professional agent, and that the communications he so makes to
him should be kept secret, unless with his consent (for it is his privilege and not the
privilege of the confidential agent)..." per Jessell M.R. in *Anderson v. Bank of British
Columbia* (1876), L.R. 2 Ch.D. 644 at 649 (C.A.). In *Maranda v. Richer*, [2003] 3
S.C.R. 193 the Supreme Court of Canada held that a lawyer's account for fees and
disbursements is protected by solicitor-client privilege.

[6] N.B. 5-C.2; N.S. 5.1; Ont. 2.03(1) Commentary. The Supreme Court of Canada
has affirmed that solicitor-client privilege must remain as close to absolute as
possible if it is to retain relevance: *Lavallee, Rackel & Heintz v. Attorney General of
Canada*, [2002] 3 S.C.R. 209 at para. 36. In the same case (at para. 24) the Court
observed that lawyers are the gatekeepers who protect the privileged information
provided by their clients.

[7] N.B. 5-C.3; N.S. 5.2; Ont. 2.03(1) Commentary.

[8] N.S. 5.3; Ont. 2.03(1) Commentary. "...a fundamental rule, namely the duty of a
solicitor to refrain from disclosing confidential information unless his client waives
the privilege.... Because the solicitor owes to his former client a duty to claim the
privilege when applicable, it is improper for him not to claim it without showing
that it has been properly waived," per Spence J. in *Bell et al. v. Smith et al.*, [1968]
S.C.R. 644 at 671. To waive the privilege, the client must know of his rights and
show a clear intention to forgo them: *Kulchar v. March & Benkert* (1950), 1 W.W.R.
272 (Sask. K.B.).

[9] N.B. 5-C.5; N.S. 5.6; Ont. 2.03(1) Commentary.

[10] N.B. 5-C.6; N.S. 5.7, 5.8; Ont. 2.03(1) Commentary.

[11] N.S. 5.9; Ont. 2.03(1) Commentary.

[12] Alta. 7-R.8(e); ABA-MC EC4-2, DR4-101(C)(1), (D); ABA-MR 1.6[5]; B.C.
5(11); N.B. 5-C.9(a); N.S. 5.10; Ont. 2.03(1) Commentary. "When a solicitor files
an affidavit on behalf of his client...it should be assumed, until the contrary is

proved, or at least until the solicitor's authority to do so is disputed by the client, that the solicitor has the authority to make the disclosure," per Lebel J. in *Kennedy v. Diversified* (1949), 1 D.L.R. 59 at 61 (Ont. H.C.).

[13] Alta. 7-R.6(a); ABA-MC EC4-5; B.C. 5(5) to 5(8); N.S. 5.4, 5.5; Ont. 2.03(b) and Commentary. Misuse by a lawyer for his own benefit of his client's confidential information may render the lawyer liable to account: *McMaster v. Byrne* (1952), 3 D.L.R. 337 (P.C.); *Bailey v. Ornheim* (1962), 40 W.W.R. (N.S.) 129 (B.C.S.C.).

[14] Alta. 7-R.8(b); ABA-MC DR4-101(C)(2); ABA-MR 1.6 [13], [14]; B.C. 5(13), 5(14); Ont. 2.03(2).

[15] Ont. 2.03(3) Commentary.

CHAPTER V

IMPARTIALITY AND CONFLICT OF INTEREST BETWEEN CLIENTS

RULE

The lawyer shall not advise or represent both sides of a dispute and, except after adequate disclosure to and with the consent of the clients or prospective clients concerned, shall not act or continue to act in a matter when there is or is likely to be a conflicting interest.[1]

Commentary

Guiding Principles

1.   A conflicting interest is one that would be likely to affect adversely the lawyer's judgment on behalf of, advice to, or loyalty to a client or prospective client.[2]

2.   The reason for the Rule is self-evident. The client or the client's affairs may be seriously prejudiced unless the lawyer's judgment and freedom of action on the client's behalf are as free as possible from compromising influences.[3]

3.   Conflicting interests include, but are not limited to, the duties and loyalties of the lawyer or a partner or professional associate of the lawyer to another client, whether involved in the particular matter or not, including the obligation to

communicate information.[4]

4.   A lawyer may not represent one client whose interests are
directly adverse to the immediate interests of another current
client, even if the two matters are unrelated, unless both
clients consent after receiving full disclosure and, preferably,
independent legal advice.

Disclosure of Conflicting Interest

5.   The Rule requires adequate disclosure to enable the client
to make an informed decision about whether to have the
lawyer act despite the existence or possibility of a conflicting
interest. As important as it is to the client that the lawyer's
judgment and freedom of action on the client's behalf should
not be subject to other interests, duties or obligations, in
practice this factor may not always be decisive. Instead it may
be only one of several factors that the client will weigh when
deciding whether to give the consent referred to in the Rule.
Other factors might include, for example, the availability of
another lawyer of comparable expertise and experience, the
extra cost, delay and inconvenience involved in engaging
another lawyer and the latter's unfamiliarity with the client
and the client's affairs. In the result, the client's interests may
sometimes be better served by not engaging another lawyer.
An example of this sort of situation is when the client and
another party to a commercial transaction are continuing
clients of the same law firm but are regularly represented by
different lawyers in that firm.[5]

6.   Before the lawyer accepts employment from more than
one client in the same matter, the lawyer must advise the
clients that the lawyer has been asked to act for both or all of
them, that no information received in connection with the
matter from one can be treated as confidential so far as any of
the others is concerned and that, if a dispute develops that

cannot be resolved, the lawyer cannot continue to act for both or all of them with respect to the matter and may have to withdraw completely. Where a lawyer has a continuing relationship with a client for whom the lawyer acts regularly, before the lawyer accepts joint employment for that client and another client in a matter or transaction, the lawyer must advise the other client of the continuing relationship and recommend that the other client obtain independent legal advice about the joint retainer. If, following such disclosure, all parties are content that the lawyer act for them, the lawyer should obtain their consent, preferably in writing, or record their consent in a separate letter to each. The lawyer should, however, guard against acting for more than one client where, despite the fact that all parties concerned consent, it is reasonably obvious that a contentious issue may arise between them or that their interests, rights or obligations will diverge as the matter progresses.[6]

7.   Although commentary 6 does not require that, before accepting a joint retainer, a lawyer advise each client to obtain independent legal advice about the joint retainer, in some cases, especially those in which one of the clients is less sophisticated or more vulnerable than the other, the lawyer should recommend doing so to ensure that the less sophisticated or more vulnerable client's consent to the joint retainer is informed, genuine, and uncoerced.[7]

8.   If a contentious issue arises between clients on a joint retainer, the lawyer, although not necessarily precluded from advising them on other non-contentious matters, would be in breach of the Rule if the lawyer attempted to advise them on the contentious issue. In such circumstances the lawyer should ordinarily refer the clients to other lawyers. However, if the issue is one that involves little or no legal advice, for example, a business rather than a legal question in a proposed business transaction, and the clients are sophisticated, they

may be permitted to settle the issue by direct negotiation in which the lawyer does not participate. Alternatively, the lawyer may refer one client to another lawyer and continue to advise the other if it was agreed at the outset that this course would be followed if a conflicting interest arose.[8]

Lawyer as Arbitrator

9.   The Rule will not prevent a lawyer from arbitrating or settling, or attempting to arbitrate or settle, a dispute between two or more clients or former clients who are *sui juris* and who wish to submit to the lawyer.[9]

Prohibition Against Acting for Borrower and Lender

10.   Subject to commentary 11, a lawyer or two or more lawyers practising in partnership or association should not act for or otherwise represent both lender and borrower in a mortgage or loan transaction.[10]

11.   A lawyer may act for or otherwise represent both lender and borrower in a mortgage or loan transaction if:

(a)   the lawyer practises in a remote location where there is no other lawyer whom either party could conveniently retain for the matter;
(b)   the lender is selling real property to the borrower and the mortgage represents part of the purchase price;
(c)   the lender is a bank, trust company, insurance company, credit union or finance company that lends money in the ordinary course of its business;
(d)   the consideration for the mortgage or loan does not exceed $50,000; or
(e)   the lender and borrower are not at "arm's length" as defined in the *Income Tax Act* (Canada).[11]

Acting Against Former Client

12. A lawyer who has acted for a client in a matter should not thereafter, in the same or any related matter, act against the client (or against a person who was involved in or associated with the client in that matter) or take a position where the lawyer might be tempted or appear to be tempted to breach the Rule relating to confidential information. It is not, however, improper for the lawyer to act against a former client in a fresh and independent matter wholly unrelated to any work the lawyer has previously done for that person.[12]

13. For the sake of clarity the foregoing paragraphs are expressed in terms of the individual lawyer and client. However, the term "client" includes a client of the law firm of which the *lawyer* is a partner or associate, whether or not the lawyer handles the client's work. It also includes the client of a lawyer who is associated with the lawyer in such a manner that they are perceived as practising in partnership or association, even though in fact no such partnership or association exists.[13]

Acting for More Than One Client

14. In practice, there are many situations where persons have a conflicting interest even though no actual dispute exists between them. A common example in a conveyancing practice is where the lawyer is asked to represent both vendor and purchaser. In cases where the lawyer is asked to act for more than one party in such a transaction, the lawyer should recommend that each party be separately represented. In all such transactions the lawyer must observe the rules prescribed by the governing body.

15. There are also many situations where more than one person may wish to retain the lawyer to handle a transaction

and, although their interests appear to coincide, a conflicting interest potentially exists. An example would be persons forming a partnership or corporation. Those cases will be governed by commentaries 5, 6 and 7 of this Chapter.

16. A lawyer who is employed or retained by an organization represents that organization through its duly authorized constituents. In dealing with the organization's directors, officers, employees, members, shareholders or other constituents, the lawyer must make clear that it is the organization that is the client whenever it becomes apparent that the organization's interests are adverse to those of a constituent with whom the lawyer is dealing. The lawyer representing an organization may also represent any of its directors, officers, employees, members, shareholders or other constituents, subject to the provisions of this Chapter.

Requests for Proposals and Other Enquiries

17. Prospective clients often interview or seek proposals from several firms about potential retainers. During the course of such a process, a prospective client may provide confidential information about the potential retainer. As a result, there is a risk that it will be suggested that a lawyer who unsuccessfully participates in such a process should be disqualified from acting for another party to the matter. Discussing a potential retainer with a prospective client or participating in a request for proposals process does not itself preclude a lawyer from acting in the matter for another party. Where the prospective client wishes to disclose confidential information as part of such a process, the lawyer and the prospective client should expressly agree whether the disclosure will prevent the lawyer from acting for another party in the matter if the lawyer is not retained by the prospective client. If the prospective client and the lawyer are unable to agree, the lawyer should insist that the prospective client not disclose confidential information

unless and until the lawyer is retained.

Confidential Government Information

18. A lawyer who has information known to be confidential government information about a person, acquired when the lawyer was a public officer or employee, shall not represent a client (other than the agency of which the lawyer was a public officer or employee) whose interests are adverse to that person in a matter in which the information could be used to that person's material disadvantage.[143]

Burden of Proof

19. Generally speaking, in disciplinary proceedings arising from a breach of this Rule the lawyer has the burden of showing good faith and that adequate disclosure was made in the matter and the client's consent was obtained.[15]

Conflicts Arising as a Result of Transfer Between Law Firms

Definitions

20. In this commentary:

"client" includes anyone to whom a member owes a duty of confidentiality, whether or not a solicitor-client relationship exists between them;

"confidential information" means information obtained from a client which is not generally known to the public;

"law firm" includes one or more members practising,

    (a)   in a sole proprietorship,

    (b)   in a partnership,

(c) in association for the purpose of sharing certain common expenses but otherwise as independent practitioners,

(d) as a professional law corporation,

(e) in a government, a Crown corporation or other public body, and

(f) in some other corporation or body.

"matter" means a case or client file, but does not include general "know-how" and, in the case of a government lawyer, does not include policy unrelated to a particular case;

"member" means a member of a law society, and includes an articled law student registered in a governing body's pre-call training program.

Application of Commentary

21. This commentary applies where a member transfers from one law firm ("former law firm") to another ("new law firm"),[16] and either the transferring member or the new law firm is aware at the time of the transfer or later discovers that:

(a) the new law firm represents a client in a matter which is the same as or related to a matter in respect of which the former law firm represents its client ("former client");

(b) the interests of those clients in that matter conflict; and

(c) the transferring member actually possesses relevant information respecting that matter.[17]

22. Paragraphs 23 to 26 do not apply to a member employed by the federal, a provincial or a territorial Attorney General or Department of Justice who, after transferring from one department, ministry or agency to another, continues to be

employed by that Attorney General or Department of Justice.[18]

Firm Disqualification

23. Where the transferring member actually possesses relevant information respecting the former client that is confidential and disclosure of it to a member of the new law firm might prejudice the former client, the new law firm shall cease its representation of its client in that matter unless:

(a) the former client consents to the new law firm's continued representation of its client; or

(b) the new law firm establishes that,

(i) it is in the interests of justice that its representation of its client in the matter continue, having regard to all relevant circumstances, including,

(A) the adequacy of the measure taken under (ii),

(B) the extent of prejudice to any party,

(C) the good faith of the parties,

(D) the availability of alternative suitable counsel, and

(E) issues affecting the national or public interest; and[19]

(ii) it has taken reasonable measures to ensure that no disclosure to any member of the new law firm of the former client's confidential information will occur.[20]

Transferring Lawyer Disqualification

24. Where the transferring member actually possesses relevant information respecting the former client and, although the

information is not confidential, disclosure of it to a member of the new law firm might prejudice the former client,[21]

   (a) the member should execute an affidavit or solemn declaration to that effect, and

   (b) the new law firm should,

      (i) notify its client and the former client, or if the former client is represented in that matter by a member, notify that member, of the relevant circumstances and its intended action under this commentary, and

      (ii) deliver to the persons referred to in (i) a copy of the affidavit or solemn declaration executed under (a).[22]

25. A transferring member described in the opening clause of paragraph 23 or 24 shall not, unless the former client consents,[23]

   (a) participate in any manner in the new law firm's representation of its client in that matter, or

   (b) disclose any confidential information respecting the former client.[24]

26. No member of the new law firm shall, unless the former client consents, discuss with a transferring member described in the opening clause of paragraph 23 or 24 the new law firm's representation of its client or the former law firm's representation of the former client in that matter.[25]

Determination of Compliance

27. Anyone who has an interest in, or who represents a party in, a matter referred to in this commentary may apply to a court of competent jurisdiction for a determination of any

aspect of this commentary.[26]

Due Diligence

28. A member shall exercise due diligence in ensuring that each member and employee of the member's law firm, and each other person whose services the member has engaged:[27]

(a) complies with this commentary; and
(b) does not disclose

(i) confidences of clients of the firm, and
(ii) confidences of clients of another law firm in which the person has worked.[28]

Application

29. The purpose of this commentary is to deal with actual knowledge. Imputed knowledge does not give rise to disqualification.[29]

A. Lawyers and support staff

This commentary is intended to regulate lawyers and articled law students who transfer between law firms. It also imposes a general duty on members to exercise due diligence in the supervision of non-lawyer staff, to ensure that they comply with the commentary and with the duty not to disclose:

(a) confidences of clients of the member's firm; or
(b) confidences of clients of other law firms in which they have worked.

B. Government employees and in-house counsel

The definition of "law firm" includes one or more lawyers practising in a government, a Crown corporation, any other public body or a corporation or other entity. Thus, this commentary applies to members transferring to or from government service and into or out of an in-house counsel position, but does not extend to a purely internal transfer after which the employer remains the same.

C. Law firms with multiple offices

This commentary treats as one "law firm" such entities as the various legal services units of a government, a corporation with separate regional legal departments, an inter-provincial law firm and a legal aid program with many community law offices. The more autonomous that each unit, department, or office is, the easier it should be, in the event of a conflict, for the new firm to obtain the former client's consent, or to establish that it is in the public interest, that it continue to represent its client in the matter.

D. Practising in association

The definition of "law firm" includes one or more lawyers practising in association for the purpose of sharing certain common expenses but who are otherwise independent practitioners. This recognizes the risk that lawyers practising in association, like partners in a law firm, will share client confidences while discussing their files with one another.[30]

Matters to Consider When Interviewing a Potential Transferee

30. When a law firm considers hiring a lawyer or articled law student ("transferring member") from another law firm, the transferring member and the new law firm need to determine,

before transfer, whether any conflicts of interest will be created.

Conflicts can arise with respect to clients of the firm that the transferring member is leaving, and with respect to clients of a firm in which the transferring member worked at some earlier time.

After completing the interview process and before hiring the transferring member, the transferring member and the new law firm need first to identify all cases in which:

(a) the new law firm represents a client in a matter which is the same as or related to a matter in respect of which the former law firm represents its client;

(b) the interests of these clients in that matter conflict; and

(c) the transferring member actually possesses relevant information respecting that matter.

When these three elements exist, the transferring member is personally disqualified from representing the new client, unless the former client consents.

Second, they must determine, with respect to each such matter, whether the information that the transferring member possesses is confidential, and whether disclosure of it to a member of the new law firm might prejudice the former client.

If this element exists, then the transferring member is disqualified unless the former client consents, and the new law firm is disqualified unless the former client consents or the new law firm establishes that its continued representation is in the public interest.

In this commentary, "confidential" information refers to

information obtained from a client that is not generally known
to the public. The obligation to keep such information
confidential should be distinguished from the general ethical
duty to hold in strict confidence all information concerning
the business and affairs of the client acquired in the course of
the professional relationship, which duty applies without
regard to the nature or source of the information or to the fact
that others may share the knowledge.

In determining whether the transferring member possesses
confidential information, both the transferring member and
the new law firm need to ensure that they do not, during the
interview process itself, disclose client confidences.[31]

Matters to Consider Before Hiring a Potential Transferee

31. After completing the interview process and before hiring
the transferring member, the new law firm should determine
whether a conflict exists.

A. Where a conflict exists[32]

If the new law firm concludes that the transferring member
does actually possess relevant information respecting a former
client which is confidential and its disclosure to a member of
the new law firm might prejudice the former client, then the
new law firm will be prohibited, if the transferring member is
hired, from continuing to represent its client in the matter
unless,

> (a) the new law firm obtains the former client's consent
>   to its continued representation of its client in that
>   matter; or
> (b) the new law firm complies with paragraph 23(b) and,
>   in determining whether continued representation is in
>   the interests of justice, both clients' interests are the
>   paramount consideration.[33]

If the new law firm seeks the former client's consent to the new law firm's continuing to act it will, in all likelihood, be required to satisfy the former client that it has taken reasonable measures to ensure that no disclosure to any member of the new law firm of the former client's confidential information will occur. The former client's consent must be obtained before the transferring member is hired.

Alternatively, if the new law firm applies under paragraph 27 for a determination that it may continue to act, it bears the onus of establishing the matters referred to in paragraph 23(b). Again, this process must be completed before the transferring person is hired.

The circumstances enumerated in paragraph 23(b)(i) are drafted in broad terms to ensure that all relevant facts will be taken into account. While clauses (B) and (D) are self-explanatory, clause (E) addresses governmental concerns respecting issues of national security, cabinet confidence and obligations incumbent on Attorneys General and their agents in the administration of justice.

B. Where no conflict exists

If the new law firm concludes that the transferring member actually possesses relevant information respecting a former client, but that information is not confidential information, which, if disclosed to a member of the new law firm, might prejudice the former client, then,

(a) the transferring member should execute an affidavit or solemn declaration to that effect; and

(b) the new law firm must notify its client and the former client/former law firm "of the relevant circumstances and its intended action under this commentary", and

deliver to them a copy of any affidavit or solemn
declaration executed by the transferring member.

Although this commentary does not require that the notice be
in writing, it would be prudent for the new law firm to
confirm these matters in writing.

The new law firm might, for example, seek the former client's
consent that the transferring member act for the new law
firm's client in the matter because in the absence of such
consent, the transferring member may not act.

If the former client does not consent that the transferring
member act, it would be prudent for the new law firm to take
reasonable measures to ensure that no disclosure to any
member of the new law firm of the former client's
confidential information will occur. If those measures are
taken, it will strengthen the new law firm's position if it is
later determined that the transferring member did in fact
possess confidential information that might prejudice the
former client.

A transferring member who possesses no such confidential
information, by executing an affidavit or solemn declaration to
that effect and delivering it to the former client, puts the
former client on notice. A former client who disputes the
allegation that there is no such confidential information may
apply under paragraph 27 for a determination of that issue.[34]

Reasonable Measures to Ensure Non-Disclosure of
Confidential Information

32. As noted above, there are two circumstances in which the
new law firm should consider the implementation of
reasonable measures to ensure that no disclosure to any
member of the new law firm of the former client's

confidential information will occur:

(a) where the transferring member actually possesses confidential information respecting a former client, disclosure of which to a member of the new law firm might prejudice the former client; and

(b) where the new law firm is not sure whether the transferring member actually possesses such confidential information, but wants to strengthen its position if it is later determined that the transferring member did in fact possess such confidential information.

It is not possible to offer a set of "reasonable measures" that will be appropriate or adequate in every case. Rather, the new law firm which seeks to implement reasonable measure must exercise professional judgment in determining what steps must be taken "to ensure that no disclosure to any member of the new law firm of the former client's confidential information will occur."

In the case of law firms with multiple offices, the degree of autonomy possessed by each office will be an important factor in determining what constitutes "reasonable measures". For example, the various legal services units of a government, a corporation with separate regional legal departments, an inter-provincial law firm or a legal aid program may be able to argue that, because of its institutional structure, reporting relationships, function, nature of work and geography, relatively fewer "measures" are necessary to ensure the non-disclosure of client confidences.

The guidelines at the end of this commentary, adapted from the Canadian Bar Association's Task Force report, entitled *Conflict of Interest Disqualification: Martin v. Gray and Screening Methods* (February 1993), are intended as a checklist of relevant factors to be considered. Adoption of only some of the guidelines may be adequate in some cases, while adoption of them all may not be sufficient in others.

Where a transferring lawyer joining a government legal services unit or the legal department of a corporation actually possesses confidential information respecting a former client, which, if disclosed to a member of the new "law firm", might prejudice the former client, the interests of the new client (i.e. Her Majesty or the corporation) must continue to be represented. Normally, this will be effected either by instituting satisfactory screening measures or, when necessary, by referring conduct of the matter to outside counsel. As each situation will be unique, flexibility will be required in the application of subparagraph 23(b), particularly clause (E).[35]

Guidelines[36]

1.   The screened member should have no involvement in the new law firm's representation of its client.

2.   The screened member should not discuss the current matter or any information relating to the representation of the former client (the two may be identical) with anyone else in the new law firm.

3.   No member of the new law firm should discuss the current matter or the prior representation with the screened member.

4.   The current matter should be discussed only within the limited group that is working on the matter.

5.   The files of the current client, including computer files, should be physically segregated from the new law firm's regular filing system, specifically identified, and accessible only

to those lawyers and support staff in the new law firm who are working on the matter or who require access for other specifically identified and approved reasons.

6. No member of the new law firm should show the screened member any document relating to the current matter.

7. The measures to be taken by the new law firm to screen the transferring member should be stated in a written policy explained to all the firm's lawyers and support staff, supported by an admonition that violation of the policy will result in sanctions, up to and including dismissal.

8. Affidavits should be provided by the appropriate firm members, setting out that they have adhered to and will continue to adhere to all elements of the screen.

9. The former client, or if the former client is represented in that matter by a member, that member, should be advised,

(a) that the screened member is now with the new law firm, which represents the current client, and

(b) of the measures adopted by the new law firm to ensure that there will be no disclosure of confidential information.

10. The screened member's office or work station and that of the member's secretary should be located away from the offices and work stations of lawyers and support staff working on the matter.

11. The screened member should use associates and support staff other than those working on the current matter.

1 Alta. 6-S.O.P., 6-R.1; ABA-MC EC5-14, 5-15, DRs 5-101(A), 5-105; ABA-MR 1.7, 1.8, 1.9; B.C. 6(1) to 6(3); N.B. 6-R, 6-C.1; N.S. 6; Ont. 2.04(2); Que. 3.06.06.

2 Ont. 2.04(1); N.S. 6-1; Que. 3.06.07; M.M. Orkin, *Legal Ethics: A Study of Professional Conduct* (Toronto: Cartwright & Jane, 1957) at pp. 98-101.

3 Ont. 2.04(3) Commentary.

4 Two fundamental duties underlie any analysis of conflict of interest problems: the duty of confidentiality and the duty of loyalty. The Supreme Court of Canada emphasized the former in *MacDonald Estate v. Martin*, [1990] 3 S.C.R. 1235 and the latter in *R. v. Neil*, [2002] 3 S.C.R. 631. See also *Bolkiah v. KPMG*, [1999] 2 A.C. 222 (H.L.).

5 Alta. 6-R.2; ABA-MC EC 5-16, 5-19; ABA-MR 1.7 (b)(4); Ont. 2.04(3) Commentary.

6 B.C. 6(4); N.B. 6-C.1(C), 6-C.2; N.S. 6-2, 6-3; Ont. 2.04(6), 2.04(7) Commentary.

7 Ont. 2.04(6) Commentary.

8 B.C. 6(5); N.S. 6-4; Ont. 2.04(9).

9 N.B. 6-C.5; N.S. 6-6; Ont. 2.04(9).

10 Ont. 2.04(11).

11 Ont. 2.04(12).

12 Alta. 6-R.3; N.B. 6-C.4; N.S. 6-8, 6-9; Ont. 2.04(4).

13 Ont. 2.04(5) Commentary.

14 B.C. 5(9), 5(10).

15 N.B. 6-C.8; N.S. C-6.8.

16 N.B. 6-C.7.

17 Alta. 6-R.4; ABA-MR 1.9(b), (c); B.C. 6(7.2); N.S. 6a-2; Ont. 2.05(2).

18 B.C. 6(7.3); N.S. 6a-3; Ont. 2.05(3).

19 Ont. 2.05(4).

20 B.C. 6(7.4); N.S. 6a-4.

21 N.S. 6a-5; Ont. 2.05(6).

22 B.C. 6(7.5).

23 N.S. 6a-6; Ont. 2.05(7).

24 B.C. 6(7.6).

25 B.C. 6(7.7); N.S. 6a-7; Ont. 2.05(8).

26 B.C. 6(7.8); Ont. 2.05(9).

27 N.S. 6a-8.

28 B.C. 6(7.9); Ont. 2.05 (10); Que. 3.06.04.

29 Ont. 2.05(3) Commentary.

30 N.S. C-6A.1.

31 B.C. Appendix 5(1); N.S. C-6A.2; Ont. 2.05(10) Commentary.

32 N.S. C-6A.3; Ont. 2.05(10) Commentary; Alta. 6-R.4(d).

33 B.C. Appendix 5(2)(a); N.S. C-6A.3(a).

34 Alta. 6-R.4(c); B.C. Appendix 5(2)(b); N.S. C-6A.3(b).

35 B.C. Appendix 5(3); N.S. C-6A.4 ; Ont. 2.05(10) Commentary.

36 B.C. Appendix 5 Guidelines; N.S. 6 Guidelines; Ont. 2.05(10) Commentary.

CHAPTER VI

CONFLICT OF INTEREST BETWEEN LAWYER AND CLIENT

RULE

1. The lawyer should not enter into a business transaction with the client or knowingly give to or acquire from the client an ownership, security or other pecuniary interest unless:[1]

   (a) the transaction is a fair and reasonable one and its terms are fully disclosed to the client in writing in a manner that is reasonably understood by the client;[2]
   (b) the client is given a reasonable opportunity to seek independent legal advice about the transaction, the onus being on the lawyer to prove that the client's interests were protected by such independent advice; and
   (c) the client consents in writing to the transaction.[3]

2. The lawyer shall not enter into or continue a business transaction with the client if:

   (a) the client expects or might reasonably be assumed to expect that the lawyer is protecting the client's interests;[4]
   (b) there is a significant risk that the interests of the lawyer and the client may differ.[5]

3. The lawyer shall not act for the client where the lawyer's duty to the client and the personal interests of the lawyer or an associate are in conflict.[6]

4. The lawyer shall not prepare an instrument giving the lawyer or an associate a substantial gift from the client, including a testamentary gift.[7]

5. The lawyer must comply with the terms of all professional liability insurance policies.[8]

Commentary

Guiding Principles

1. The principles enunciated in the Rule relating to impartiality and conflict of interest between clients apply *mutatis mutandis* to this Rule.

2. A conflict of interest between lawyer and client exists in all cases where the lawyer gives property to or acquires it from the client by way of purchase, gift, testamentary disposition or otherwise. Such transactions are to be avoided. When they are contemplated, the prudent course is to insist that the client either be independently represented or have independent legal advice.[9]

3. This Rule applies also to situations involving associates of the lawyer. Associates of the lawyer within the meaning of the Rule include the lawyer's spouse, children, any relative of the lawyer (or of the lawyer's spouse) living under the same roof, any partner or associate of the lawyer in the practice of law, a trust or estate in which the lawyer has a substantial beneficial interest or for which the lawyer acts as a trustee or in a similar capacity, and a corporation of which the lawyer is a director or in which the lawyer or an associate owns or controls, directly

or indirectly, a significant number of shares.[10]

Debtor-Creditor Relationship to be Avoided

4. The lawyer should avoid entering into a debtor-creditor relationship with the client. The lawyer should not borrow money from a client who is not in the business of lending money. It is undesirable that the lawyer lend money to the client except by way of advancing necessary expenses in a legal matter that the lawyer is handling for the client.[11]

Joint Ventures

5. The lawyer who has a personal interest in a joint business venture with others may represent or advise the business venture in legal matters between it and third parties, but should not represent or advise either the joint business venture or the joint venturers in respect of legal matters as between them.

When Person to be Considered a Client

6. The question of whether a person is to be considered a client of the lawyer when such person is lending money to the lawyer, or buying, selling, making a loan to or investment in, or assuming an obligation in respect of a business, security or property in which the lawyer or an associate of the lawyer has an interest, or in respect of any other transaction, is to be determined having regard to all the circumstances. A person who is not otherwise a client may be deemed to be a client for purposes of this Rule if such person might reasonably feel entitled to look to the lawyer for guidance and advice in respect of the transaction. In those circumstances the lawyer must consider such person to be a client and will be bound by the same fiduciary obligations that attach to a lawyer in dealings with a client. The onus shall be on the lawyer to

establish that such a person was not in fact looking to the
lawyer for guidance and advice.[12]

---

[1] ABA-MC Canon 5, DR 5-101(A), (B); ABA-MR 1.8(a); Ont. 2.06(2).
[2] N.S. 7(c)(ii).
[3] Alta. 6-R.9; N.B. 11-R(a); N.S. 7(c)(iii).
[4] N.B. 11-R(b).
[5] N.S. 7(b).
[6] N.S. 7(a).
[7] ABA-MR 1.8(c); N.S. 7(f).
[8] Alta. 6-R.8; B.C. 7.
[9] N.S. R-7(e); Que. 3.05.13.
[10] As to corporations, cf. ABA EC 5-18: "A lawyer employed or retained by a
corporation or similar entity owes his allegiance to the entity and not to a
stockholder, director, officer, employee, representative, or other person connected
with the entity. In advising the entity, a lawyer should keep paramount its
interests...".
[11] Ont. 2.06(4)(a); Que. 3.05.12.
[12] N.B. 11-C.6; N.S. C-7.1.

CHAPTER VII

OUTSIDE INTERESTS AND THE PRACTICE OF LAW

RULE

The lawyer who engages in another profession, business or occupation concurrently with the practice of law must not allow such outside interest to jeopardize the lawyer's professional integrity, independence or competence.[1]

Commentary

Guiding Principles

1.   The term "outside interest" covers the widest possible range and includes activities that may overlap or be connected with the practice of law, such as engaging in the mortgage business, acting as a director of a client corporation, or writing on legal subjects, as well as activities not so connected such as a career in business, politics, broadcasting or the performing arts. In each case the question of whether the lawyer may properly engage in the outside interest and to what extent will be subject to any applicable law or rule of the governing body.[2]

2.   Whenever an overriding social, political, economic or other consideration arising from the outside interest might influence the lawyer's judgment, the lawyer should be governed by the considerations declared in the Rule relating to

conflict of interest between lawyer and client.[3]

3. Where the outside interest is in no way related to the legal services being performed for clients, ethical considerations will usually not arise unless the lawyer's conduct brings either the lawyer or the profession into disrepute or impairs the lawyer's competence as, for example, where the outside interest occupies so much time that clients suffer because of the lawyer's lack of attention or preparation.[4]

4. The lawyer must not carry on, manage or be involved in any outside business, investment, property or occupation in such a way that makes it difficult to distinguish in which capacity the lawyer is acting in a particular transaction, or that would give rise to a conflict of interest or duty to a client. When acting or dealing in respect of a transaction involving an outside interest in a business, investment, property or occupation, the lawyer must disclose any personal interest, must declare to all parties in the transaction or to their solicitors whether the lawyer is acting on the lawyer's own behalf or in a professional capacity or otherwise, and must adhere throughout the transaction to standards of conduct as high as those that this Code requires of a lawyer engaged in the practice of law.[5]

5. The lawyer who has an outside interest in a business, investment, property or occupation:

  (a) must not be identified as a lawyer when carrying on, managing or being involved in such outside interest; and
  (b) must ensure that monies received in respect of the day-to-day carrying on, operation and management of such outside interest are deposited in an account other than the lawyer's trust account, unless such monies are received by the lawyer when acting in a

professional capacity as a lawyer on behalf of the outside interest.

6. In order to be compatible with the practice of law the other profession, business or occupation:

(a) must be an honourable one that does not detract from the status of the lawyer or the legal profession generally; and

(b) must not be such as would likely result in a conflict of interest between the lawyer and a client.

---

[1] Alta. 15-S.O.P.; N.B. 14-R(a); Ont. 6.04(1); N.S. R-8. This Rule is closely connected with the Rule relating to conflict of interest between lawyer and client.

[2] Ont. 6.04(2) Commentary; N.S. R-8. In Quebec, s. 122(1)(b) of *An Act respecting the Barreau du Québec* provides that a person shall become disqualified from practising as an advocate when "he holds a position or an office incompatible with the practice or dignity of the profession of advocate." Que. 4.01.01(c) prohibits lawyers from having an interest in collection agencies.

[3] N.S. C-8.2.

[4] Ont. 6.04(2) Commentary; N.S. C-8.3.

[5] Alta. 15-R.1, R.3; N.S. C-8.4 to C-8.6.

[6] N.S. C-8.7.

CHAPTER VIII

PRESERVATION OF CLIENTS' PROPERTY

RULE

The lawyer owes a duty to the client to observe all relevant laws and rules respecting the preservation and safekeeping of the client's property entrusted to the lawyer. Where there are no such laws or rules, or the lawyer is in any doubt, the lawyer should take the same care of such property as a careful and prudent owner would when dealing with property of like description.[1]

Commentary

Guiding Principles

1.   The lawyer's duties with respect to safekeeping, preserving and accounting for the clients' monies and other property are generally the subject of special rules.[2] In the absence of such rules the lawyer should adhere to the minimum standards set out in note 3.[3] "Property", apart from clients' monies, includes securities such as mortgages, negotiable instruments, stocks, bonds, etc., original documents such as wills, title deeds, minute books, licences, certificates, etc., other papers such as clients' correspondence files, reports, invoices, etc., as well as chattels such as jewellery, silver, etc.

2.   The lawyer should promptly notify the client upon receiving any property of or relating to the client unless satisfied that the client knows that it has come into the lawyer's custody.[4]

3.   The lawyer should clearly label and identify the client's property and place it in safekeeping separate and apart from the lawyer's own property.[5]

4.   The lawyer should maintain adequate records of clients' property in the lawyer's custody so that it may be promptly accounted for, or delivered to, or to the order of, the client upon request. The lawyer should ensure that such property is delivered to the right person and, in case of dispute as to the person entitled, may have recourse to the courts.[6]

5.   The duties here expressed are closely related to those concerning confidential information.[7] The lawyer should keep clients' papers and other property out of sight as well as out of reach of those not entitled to see them and should, subject to any right of lien,[8] return them promptly to the clients upon request or at the conclusion of the lawyer's retainer.[9]

Privilege

6.   The lawyer should be alert to claim on behalf of clients any lawful privilege respecting information about their affairs, including their files and property if seized or attempted to be seized by a third party. In this regard the lawyer should be familiar with the nature of clients' privilege, and with relevant statutory provisions such as those in the *Income Tax Act,* the *Criminal Code,* the *Canadian Charter of Rights and Freedoms* and other statutes. [10]

[1] ABA-MC DR 9-102(B); ABA-MR 1.15; Alta. 7-R.3; B.C. 7.1; N.B. 7-R; N.S. R-9; Ont. 2.07(1); Que. 3.02.06 to 3.02.08. Although the basic duty here declared may parallel the legal duty under the law of bailment, it is reiterated as being a matter of professional responsibility quite apart from the position in law.

[2] ABA-MC EC 9-5, DR 9-102(A), (B); N.S. R-9 Guiding Principles.

[3] The minimum standards are:

    (a) paying into and keeping monies received or held by the lawyer for or on behalf of clients in a trust bank account or accounts separate from the bank account of the lawyer or the lawyer's firm;

    (b) keeping properly written books and accounts of all monies received, held or paid by the lawyer for or on behalf of each of the lawyer's clients which clearly distinguish such monies from the monies of every other client and from the monies of the lawyer and the lawyer's firm;

    (c) not retaining for an unnecessarily long period, without the express authority of the client, monies received for or on behalf of such client;

    (d) subject to rules prescribed by the governing body of the province, no lawyer shall take fees, as opposed to disbursements, from funds held in trust for a client without the client's express authority unless the work being done by the lawyer for the client has been performed and a proper account in respect thereof has been rendered to the client. Where a client authorizes the payment of fees from trust funds before an account has been rendered, this arrangement should be recorded in writing and an interim account sent to the client forthwith;

    (e) the lawyer should not estimate a lump sum that may in the aggregate be owed by a number of clients and then transfer that sum in bulk from a trust account to the lawyer's general account without allocating specific amounts to each client and rendering an account to each client.

[4] ABA DR 9-102 (B)(1); N.B. 7-C.1(a); N.S. C.9.1; Ont. 2.07(2).

[5] N.B. 7-C.1(b); N.S. C-9.2; Ont. 2.07(3).

[6] N.B. 7-C.2; N.S. C-9.3, C-9.4; Ont. 2.07(4). For example, by seeking leave to interplead.

[7] Cf. the Rule relating to confidential information (Chapter IV).

[8] Cf. para. 11 of the Rule relating to withdrawal (Chapter XII). The lawyer's arrangements and procedures for the storage and eventual destruction of completed files should reflect the foregoing considerations and particularly the continuing obligation as to confidentiality. Further, statutes such as the *Income Tax Act* and the operation of limitations statutes pertinent to the client's position may preclude the destruction of files or particular papers. In several provinces statutes provide for the appointment of a custodian or trustee or the intervention of the syndic to conserve clients' property where a lawyer has died, absconded or become incapable. See, e.g., *Legal Profession Act*, R.S.B.C. 1998, c.9, s.50; *An act respecting the Barreau du Québec*, R.S.Q., c.B-1, s. 76(2); *Law Society Act*, R.S.O. 1990, c. L8, s. 49.45.

[9] N.B. 7-C.3; N.S. C-9.5, 9.6; Ont. 2.07(1) Commentary.

[10] N.B. 7-C.4; Ont. 2.07(6) Commentary.

CHAPTER IX

THE LAWYER AS ADVOCATE

RULE

When acting as an advocate, the lawyer must treat the court or tribunal with courtesy and respect and must represent the client resolutely, honourably and within the limits of the law.[1]

Commentary

Guiding Principles

1. The advocate's duty to the client "fearlessly to raise every issue, advance every argument, and ask every question, however distasteful, which he thinks will help his client's case" and to endeavour "to obtain for his client the benefit of any and every remedy and defence which is authorized by law"[2] must always be discharged by fair and honourable means, without illegality and in a manner consistent with the lawyer's duty to treat the court with candour, fairness, courtesy and respect.[3]

Prohibited Conduct

2. The lawyer must not, for example:

   (a) abuse the process of the tribunal by instituting or prosecuting proceedings that, although legal in themselves, are clearly motivated by malice on the part of the client and are brought solely for the purpose of injuring another party;[4]

(b) knowingly assist or permit the client to do anything that the lawyer considers to be dishonest or dishonourable;[5]

(c) appear before a judicial officer when the lawyer, the lawyer's associates or the client have business or personal relationships with such officer that give rise to real or apparent pressure, influence or inducement affecting the impartiality of such officer;[6]

(d) attempt or allow anyone else to attempt, directly or indirectly, to influence the decision or actions of a tribunal or any of its officials by any means except open persuasion as an advocate;[7]

(e) knowingly attempt to deceive or participate in the deception of a tribunal or influence the course of justice by offering false evidence, misstating facts or law, presenting or relying upon a false or deceptive affidavit, suppressing what ought to be disclosed or otherwise assisting in any fraud, crime or illegal conduct;[8]

(f) knowingly misstate the contents of a document, the testimony of a witness, the substance of an argument or the provisions of a statute or like authority;[9]

(g) make suggestions to a witness recklessly or that he or she knows to be false. The cross-examiner may pursue any hypothesis that is honestly advanced on the strength of reasonable inference, experience or intuition;[10]

(h) deliberately refrain from informing the tribunal of any pertinent adverse authority that the lawyer considers to be directly in point and that has not been mentioned by an opponent;[11]

(i) dissuade a material witness from giving evidence, or advise such a witness to be absent;[12]

(j) knowingly permit a witness to be presented in a false
or misleading way or to impersonate another;[13]

(k) needlessly abuse, hector or harass a witness;[14]

(l) needlessly inconvenience a witness.[15]

Errors and Omissions

3. The lawyer who has unknowingly done or failed to do
something that, if done or omitted knowingly, would have
been in breach of this Rule and discovers it, has a duty to the
court, subject to the Rule relating to confidential information,
to disclose the error or omission and do all that can reasonably
be done in the circumstances to rectify it.[16]

Duty to Withdraw

4. If the client wishes to adopt a course that would involve a
breach of this Rule, the lawyer must refuse and do everything
reasonably possible to prevent it. If the client persists in such a
course the lawyer should, subject to the Rule relating to
withdrawal, withdraw or seek leave of the court to do so.[17]

The Lawyer as Witness

5. The lawyer who appears as an advocate should not submit
the lawyer's own affidavit to or testify before a tribunal save as
permitted by local rule or practice, or as to purely formal or
uncontroverted matters. This also applies to the lawyer's
partners and associates; generally speaking, they should not
testify in such proceedings except as to merely formal matters.
The lawyer should not express personal opinions or beliefs, or
assert as fact anything that is properly subject to legal proof,
cross-examination or challenge. The lawyer must not in effect
become an unsworn witness or put the lawyer's own
credibility in issue. The lawyer who is a necessary witness
should testify and entrust the conduct of the case to someone

else. Similarly, the lawyer who was a witness in the proceedings should not appear as advocate in any appeal from the decision in those proceedings.[18] There are no restrictions upon the advocate's right to cross-examine another lawyer, and the lawyer who does appear as a witness should not expect to receive special treatment by reason of professional status.

Interviewing Witnesses

6. The lawyer may properly seek information from any potential witness (whether under subpoena or not) but should disclose the lawyer's interest and take care not to subvert or suppress any evidence or procure the witness to stay out of the way.[19] The lawyer shall not approach or deal with an opposite party who is professionally represented save through or with the consent of that party's lawyer.[20]

A lawyer retained to act on a matter involving a corporation or organization that is represented by another lawyer should not approach

(a) a director, officer, or person likely involved in the decision-making process for the corporation or organization, or

(b) an employee or agent of the corporation or organization whose acts or omissions in connection with the matter may have exposed it to civil or criminal liability, concerning that matter,

except to the extent that the lawyer representing the corporation or organization consents or as otherwise authorized or required by law. [21]

Unmeritorious Proceedings

7. The lawyer should never waive or abandon the client's

legal rights (for example, an available defence under a statute of limitations) without the client's informed consent. In civil matters it is desirable that the lawyer should avoid and discourage the client from resorting to frivolous or vexatious objections or attempts to gain advantage from slips or oversights not going to the real merits, or tactics that will merely delay or harass the other side. Such practices can readily bring the administration of justice and the legal profession into disrepute.[22]

Encouraging Settlements and Alternative Dispute Resolution

8.   Whenever the case can be settled reasonably, the lawyer should advise and encourage the client to do so rather than commence or continue legal proceedings. The lawyer should consider the use of alternative dispute resolution (ADR) for every dispute and, if appropriate, the lawyer should inform the client of the ADR options and, if so instructed, take steps to pursue those options.[23]

Duties of Prosecutor

9.   When engaged as a prosecutor, the lawyer's prime duty is not to seek a conviction, but to present before the trial court all available credible evidence relevant to the alleged crime in order that justice may be done through a fair trial upon the merits. The prosecutor exercises a public function involving much discretion and power and must act fairly and dispassionately. The prosecutor should not do anything that might prevent the accused from being represented by counsel or communicating with counsel and, to the extent required by law and accepted practice, should make timely disclosure to the accused or defence counsel (or to the court if the accused is not represented) of all relevant facts and known witnesses, whether tending to show guilt or innocence, or that would affect the punishment of the accused.[24] There is a clear

distinction between prosecutorial discretion and professional conduct. Only the latter can be regulated by a law society. A law society has jurisdiction to investigate any alleged breach of its ethical standards, even those committed by Crown prosecutors in connection with their prosecutorial discretion.

Duties of Defence Counsel

10. When defending an accused person, the lawyer's duty is to protect the client as far as possible from being convicted except by a court of competent jurisdiction and upon legal evidence sufficient to support a conviction for the offence charged. Accordingly, and notwithstanding the lawyer's private opinion as to credibility or merits, the lawyer may properly rely upon all available evidence or defences including so-called technicalities not known to be false or fraudulent.[25]

11. Admissions made by the accused to the lawyer may impose strict limitations on the conduct of the defence and the accused should be made aware of this. For example, if the accused clearly admits to the lawyer the factual and mental elements necessary to constitute the offence, the lawyer, if convinced that the admissions are true and voluntary, may properly take objection to the jurisdiction of the court, or to the form of the indictment, or to the admissibility or sufficiency of the evidence, but must not suggest that some other person committed the offence, or call any evidence that, by reason of the admissions, the lawyer believes to be false. Nor may the lawyer set up an affirmative case inconsistent with such admissions, for example, by calling evidence in support of an alibi intended to show that the accused could not have done, or in fact had not done, the act. Such admissions will also impose a limit upon the extent to which the lawyer may attack the evidence for the prosecution. The lawyer is entitled to test the evidence given by each individual witness for the prosecution and argue that the evidence taken

as a whole is insufficient to amount to proof that the accused is guilty of the offence charged, but the lawyer should go no further than that.[26]

12. A lawyer representing an accused or potential accused must not take unfair or improper advantage of an unrepresented complainant by attempting to influence the complainant or potential complainant with respect to the laying, prosecution or withdrawal of a criminal charge.

Agreement on Guilty Plea

13. Where, following investigation,

    (a) the defence lawyer *bona fide* concludes and advises the accused client that an acquittal of the offence charged is uncertain or unlikely,

    (b) the client is prepared to admit the necessary factual and mental elements,[27]

    (c) the lawyer fully advises the client of the implications and possible consequences of a guilty plea and that the matter of sentence is solely in the discretion of the trial judge, and

    (d) the client so instructs the lawyer, preferably in writing,[28]

it is proper for the lawyer to discuss and agree tentatively with the prosecutor to enter a plea of guilty on behalf of the client to the offence charged or to a lesser or included offence or to another offence appropriate to the admissions, and also on a disposition or sentence to be proposed to the court. The public interest and the client's interests must not, however, be compromised by agreeing to a guilty plea.[29]

Undertakings

14. An undertaking given by the lawyer to the court or to another lawyer in the course of litigation or other adversary proceedings must be strictly and scrupulously carried out. Unless clearly qualified in writing, the lawyer's undertaking is a personal promise and responsibility.[30]

Discovery Obligations

15. Where the rules of a court or tribunal require the parties to produce documents or attend on examinations for discovery, a lawyer, when acting as an advocate, shall explain to the client the necessity of making full disclosure of all documents relating to any matter in issue, and the duty to answer to the best of the client's knowledge, information, and belief, any proper question relating to any issue in the action or made discoverable by the rules of court or the rules of the tribunal; shall assist the client in fulfilling the obligation to make full disclosure, and shall not make frivolous requests for the production of documents or make frivolous demands for information at the examination for discovery.

Courtesy

16. The lawyer should at all times be courteous, civil, and act in good faith to the court or tribunal and to all persons with whom the lawyer has dealings in the course of an action or proceeding. Legal contempt of court and the professional obligation outlined here are not identical, and a consistent pattern of rude, provocative or disruptive conduct by the lawyer, even though not punished as contempt, might well merit disciplinary action.[31]

Role in Adversary Proceedings

17. In adversary proceedings, the lawyer's function as advocate is openly and necessarily partisan. Accordingly, the lawyer is not obliged (save as required by law or under paragraphs 2(h) or 7 above) to assist an adversary or advance matters derogatory to the client's case. When opposing interests are not represented, for example, in *ex parte* or uncontested matters, or in other situations where the full proof and argument inherent in the adversary system cannot be obtained, the lawyer must take particular care to be accurate, candid and comprehensive in presenting the client's case so as to ensure that the court is not misled.[32]

Communicating with Witnesses

18. When in court the lawyer should observe local rules and practices concerning communication with a witness about the witness's evidence or any issue in the proceeding. Generally, it is considered improper for counsel who called a witness to communicate with that witness without leave of the court while such witness is under cross-examination.[33]

Agreements Guaranteeing Recovery

19. In civil proceedings the lawyer has a duty not to mislead the court about the position of the client in the adversary process. Thus, where a lawyer representing a client in litigation has made or is party to an agreement made before or during the trial whereby a plaintiff is guaranteed recovery by one or more parties notwithstanding the judgment of the court, the lawyer shall disclose full particulars of the agreement to the court and all other parties.

Scope of the Rule

20. The principles of this Rule apply generally to the lawyer as
advocate and therefore extend not only to court proceedings
but also to appearances and proceedings before boards,
administrative tribunals and other bodies, regardless of their
function or the informality of their procedures.[34]

Relations with Jurors

21. When acting as an advocate, before the trial of a case, a
lawyer should not communicate with or cause another to
communicate with anyone that the lawyer knows to be a
member of the jury panel. A lawyer may investigate a person
who is a prospective juror to ascertain any basis for challenge,
but in doing so must not directly or indirectly communicate
with that person or with any member of that person's family.
When acting as an advocate, a lawyer should disclose to the
judge and opposing counsel any information of which the
lawyer is aware that a juror or perspective juror (a) has or may
have an interest, direct or indirect, in the outcome of the case,
(b) is acquainted with or connected in any manner with the
presiding judge, any counsel or any party, or (c) is acquainted
with or connected in any manner with any person who has
appeared or who is expected to appear as a witness, unless the
judge and opposing counsel are already aware of the
information. A lawyer should promptly disclose to the court
any information of which the lawyer is aware concerning
improper conduct by a member of a jury panel or by a juror
toward another member of the panel, another juror, or a
member of a juror's family. Except as permitted by law, when
acting as an advocate, a lawyer should not during a jury trial
communicate with or cause another to communicate with any
member of the jury. A lawyer who is not connected with the
case before a jury should not communicate with or cause
another to communicate with any member of the jury about

the case. A lawyer must have no discussion with a member of
the jury about its deliberations after trial.[35]

[1] Alta. 10-S.O.P.; ABA-MC Canon 7; ABA-MR 3; N.B. 8-R; N.S. R-10; Ont.
4.01(1). "The concept that counsel is the mouth-piece of his client and that his
speech is the speech of the client is as unfortunate as it is inaccurate. He is not the
agent or delegate of his client. Within proper bounds, however, counsel must be
fearless and independent in the defence of his client's rights.... He must be
completely selfless in standing up courageously for his client's rights, and he should
never expose himself to the reproach that he has sacrificed his client's interests on
the altar of expediency..." per Schroeder J. A., "Some Ethical Problems in Criminal
Law" in Law Soc. U.C. Special Lectures (1963) 87 at 102. An additional reference is
The Advocates' Society, *Principles of Civility for Advocates* (Ontario), see Appendix.
[2] The sources of the quotations are (a) per Lord Reid in *Rondel v. Worsley* (1969) 1
A.C. 191 at 227 and (b) Canon 3(5) of the *Canons of Legal Ethics* of the Canadian Bar
Association, adopted in 1920.
[3] ABA-MC EC 7-1, 7-19; N.B. 8-R(b); N.S. R-9 Guiding Principle; Ont. 4.01(1)
Commentary.
[4] ABA-MC DR 7-102(A)(1); B.C. 8(1)(a).
[5] B.C. 8(1)(b).
[6] ABA-MC Canon 9, DR 9-101; B.C. 8(1)(c).
[7] ABA-MC EC 7-34; B.C. 8(1)(d).
[8] Alta. 10-R.14, R. 20(b); ABA-MC EC 7-25 to 7-27, DR 7-102(A)(3); ABA-MR
3.3(a)(1)(3). "The swearing of an untrue affidavit...is perhaps the most obvious
example of conduct which a solicitor cannot knowingly permit.... He cannot
properly, still less can he consistently with his duty to the Court, prepare and place a
perjured affidavit upon file.... A solicitor who has innocently put on the file an
affidavit by his client which he has subsequently discovered to be certainly false owes
it to the Court to put the matter right at the earliest date if he continues to act..." per
Viscount Maugham in *Myers v. Elman* (1940), A.C. 282 at 293-94 (H.L.).
"[Counsel] had full knowledge of the impropriety of the paragraphs in the
affidavit...[and] is bound to accept responsibility for [them].... If he knows that his
client is making false statements under oath and does nothing to correct it, his
silence indicates, at the very least, a gross neglect of duty," per McLennan J.A. in *Re
Ontario Crime Commission* (1962), 37 D.L.R. (2d) 382 at 391 (Ont. C.A.).
[9] ABA-MC DR 7-102(A)(5).
[10] Alta. 10-R.19; ABA-MC EC 7-25, DR 7-106(C)(I); B.C. 8(1)(e); *R. v. Lyttle*,
[2004] 1 S.C.R. 193.
[11] ABA-MC EC 7-23, DR 7-106(B)(1); ABA MR 3.3(a)(2); B.C. 8(1)(f). See *Glebe
Sugar v. Greenock Trustees* (1921), W.N. 85 (H.L.) for a strong statement by Lord
Birkenhead on the duty of counsel to disclose to the court authorities bearing one
way or the other: "The extreme impropriety of such a course [withholding a known
pertinent authority] could not be made too plain."

[12] ABA-MC DR 7-109(B); B.C. 8(1)(g).

[13] Alta. 10-R.24; B.C. 8(1)(h); N.B. 8-C.10.

[14] Alta. 10-R.21.

[15] Ont. 4.01(2).

[16] ABA-MC DR 7-102(B), DR 4-101 (C)(2); N.B. 8-C.11; Ont. 4.01(5).

[17] ABA-MC DR 2-110 (B)(2); ABA-MR 3.3[15]; B.C. 8(7), 8(8).

[18] ABA-MC EC 7-24, DR 7-106 (C)(3), (4); ABA-MR 3.7; B.C. 8(9), (10); N.B. 8-C.6; N.S. C-10.11; Ont. 4.02. "It is improper, in my opinion, for Counsel for the Crown to express his opinion as to the guilt or innocence of the accused. In the article to which I have referred it is said that it is because the character or eminence of a counsel is to be wholly disregarded in determining the justice or otherwise of his client's cause that it is an inflexible rule of forensic pleading that an advocate shall not, as such, express his personal opinion of or his belief in his client's cause," per Locke J. in *Boucher v. The Queen*, [1955] S.C.R. 16 at 26.

[19] ABA-MC DR 7-109; B.C. 8(12), (12.2), (12.3); N.B. 8-C.4 (a), (b); Ont. 4.03(1).

[20] ABA-MC DR 7-104(A)(1); B.C. 8(12.1); N.B. 8-C.4(c); Ont. 4.03(2).

[21] Ont. 4.03(3).

[22] ABA-MC EC 7-38, 7-39, DR 7-106(C)(5); N.B. 8-C.7, C.8; N.S. C-10.1.

[23] N.B. 8-C.1, C.2(a), (b); N.S. C-10.2, 10.2A.

[24] Alta. 10-R.28; ABA-MC EC 7-13, 7-14, DR 7-103; ABA-MR 3.8; B.C. 8(18); N.B. 8-C.13; Ont. 4.01(3). "It cannot be overemphasized that the purpose of a criminal prosecution is not to obtain a conviction, it is to lay before the jury what the Crown considers to be credible evidence relevant to what is alleged to be a crime. Counsel have a duty to see that all available legal proof of the facts is presented; it should be done firmly and pressed to its legitimate strength but it must also be done fairly. The role of prosecutor excludes any notion of winning or losing; his function is a matter of public duty than which in civil life there can be none charged with greater personal responsibility. It is to be performed with an ingrained sense of the dignity, the seriousness and the justness of judicial proceedings," per Rand J. in *Boucher v. The Queen*, [1955] S.C.R. 16 at 23-24. See also Martin, "The Role and Responsibility of the Defence Advocate" (1969-70) 12 Crim. L.Q. 376 at 386-87.

[25] ABA-MC EC 7-24, DR 7-106(C)(4); N.B. 8-C.14a,b,c; N.S. C-10.3, 10.4; Ont. 4.01(1) Commentary.

[26] N.B. 8-C.14(d); N.S. C-10.5 to 10.7; Ont. 4.01(9) Commentary.

[27] ABA-MC EC 7.7; B.C. 8(20); N.B. 8-C.15; N.S. C-10.8; Ont. 4.01(9) Commentary.

[28] Alta. 10-R.27(b).

[29] Alta. 10-R.27(a).

[30] ABA-MC EC 7-38, DR 7-106(C)(5); Ont. 4.01(7) and Commentary; Ont. 4.01(5).

[31] ABA-MC EC 7-36, DR 7-106(C)(6); Ont. 4.01(6) and Commentary.

[32] ABA-MC EC 7-19; N.B. 8-C.3(a),(c); Ont. 4.01(1) Commentary.

[33] N.B. 8-C.5; Ont. 4.04 provides as follows: "Subject to the direction of the tribunal, the lawyer shall observe the following rules respecting communication with witnesses giving evidence:

    (a) during examination-in-chief, the examining lawyer may discuss with the witness any matter that has not been covered in the examination up to that point;

    (b) during examination-in-chief by another lawyer of a witness who is unsympathetic to the lawyer's cause, the lawyer not conducting the examination-in-chief may properly discuss the evidence with the witness;

    (c) between completion of examination-in-chief and commencement of cross-examination of the lawyer's own witness, the lawyer ought not to discuss the evidence given in chief or relating to any matter introduced or touched upon during the examination-in-chief;

    (d) during cross-examination by an opposing lawyer, the witness's own lawyer ought not to have any conversation with the witness about the witness's evidence or any issue in the proceeding;

    (e) between completion of cross-examination and commencement of re-examination, the lawyer who is going to re-examine the witness ought not to have any discussion about evidence that will be dealt with on re-examination;

    (f) during cross-examination by the lawyer of a witness unsympathetic to the cross-examiner's cause, the lawyer may discuss the witness's evidence with the witness;

    (g) during cross-examination by the lawyer of a witness who is sympathetic to that lawyer's cause, any conversations ought to be restricted in the same way as communications during examination-in-chief of one's own witness; and

    (h) during re-examination of a witness called by an opposing lawyer, if the witness is sympathetic to the lawyer's cause the lawyer ought not to discuss the evidence to be given by that witness during re-examination. The lawyer may, however, properly discuss the evidence with a witness who is adverse in interest.

If any question arises whether the lawyer's behaviour may be in violation of this rule, it will often be appropriate to obtain the consent of the opposing lawyer or leave of the tribunal before engaging in conversations that may be considered improper." However, "It is submitted with respect that in some respects [this commentary] may inhibit the discovery of truth and go beyond what was the practice in High Court," per Sopinka and Polin, *The Trial of an Action*, p. 106.

[34] ABA-MC EC 7-15; N.B. 8-C.16.

[35] ABA-MC EC 7-29; Ont. 4.05.

CHAPTER X

THE LAWYER IN PUBLIC OFFICE

RULE

The lawyer who holds public office should, in the discharge of official duties, adhere to standards of conduct as high as those that these rules require of a lawyer engaged in the practice of law.[1]

Commentary

Guiding Principles

1.   The Rule applies to the lawyer who is elected or appointed to legislative or administrative office at any level of government, regardless of whether the lawyer attained such office because of professional qualifications.[2] Because such a lawyer is in the public eye, the legal profession can more readily be brought into disrepute by failure on the lawyer's part to observe its professional standards of conduct.[3]

Conflicts of Interest

2.   The lawyer who holds public office must not allow personal or other interests to conflict with the proper discharge of official duties. The lawyer holding part-time public office must not accept any private legal business where duty to the client will or may conflict with official duties. If

some unforeseen conflict arises, the lawyer should terminate the professional relationship, explaining to the client that official duties must prevail. The lawyer who holds a full-time public office will not be faced with this sort of conflict, but must nevertheless guard against allowing the lawyer's independent judgment in the discharge of official duties to be influenced by the lawyer's own interest, or by the interests of persons closely related to or associated with the lawyer, or of former or prospective clients, or of former or prospective partners or associates.[4]

3.   In the context of the preceding paragraph, persons closely related to or associated with the lawyer include a spouse, child, or any relative of the lawyer (or of the lawyer's spouse) living under the same roof, a trust or estate in which the lawyer has a substantial beneficial interest or for which the lawyer acts as a trustee or in a similar capacity, and a corporation of which the lawyer is a director or in which the lawyer or some closely related or associated person holds or controls, directly or indirectly, a significant number of shares.[5]

4.   Subject to any special rules applicable to a particular public office, the lawyer holding such office who sees the possibility of a conflict of interest should declare such interest at the earliest opportunity and take no part in any consideration, discussion or vote with respect to the matter in question.[6]

Appearances before Official Bodies

5.   When the lawyer or any of the lawyer's partners or associates is a member of an official body such as, for example, a school board, municipal council or governing body, the lawyer should not appear professionally before that body. However, subject to the rules of the official body, it would not be improper for the lawyer to appear professionally before a committee of such body if such partner or associate is not a

member of that committee.[7]

6.   The lawyer should not represent in the same or any related matter any persons or interests that the lawyer has been concerned with in an official capacity. Similarly, the lawyer should avoid advising upon a ruling of an official body of which the lawyer either is a member or was a member at the time the ruling was made.

Disclosure of Confidential Information[8]

7.   By way of corollary to the Rule relating to confidential information, the lawyer who has acquired confidential information by virtue of holding public office should keep such information confidential and not divulge or use it even though the lawyer has ceased to hold such office. As to the taking of employment in connection with any matter in respect of which the lawyer had substantial responsibility or confidential information, see commentary 3 of the Rule relating to avoiding questionable conduct (Chapter XIX).[9]

Disciplinary Action

8.   Generally speaking, a governing body will not be concerned with the way in which a lawyer holding public office carries out official responsibilities, but conduct in office that reflects adversely upon the lawyer's integrity or professional competence may subject the lawyer to disciplinary action.[10]

---

[1] Alta. 12-S.O.P.; ABA-MC 8.8; DR 8-101(A); ABA-MR 1.11; N.B. 17-R; N.S. R-16; Ont. 6.05(1); Que. 3.05.09.

[2] Common examples include Senators, Members of the House of Commons, members of provincial legislatures, cabinet ministers, municipal councillors, school trustees, members and officials of boards, commissions, tribunals and departments,

commissioners of inquiry, arbitrators and mediators, Crown prosecutors and many others. For a general discussion, see Woodman, "The Lawyer in Public Life", Pitblado Lectures (Manitoba, 1971), p. 129.

[3] Ont. 6.05(1) Commentary; N.S. R-16 Guiding Principles, C-16.1.

[4] ABA-MR 1.11(d); N.B. 17-C.2(a), (b), (c); N.S. C-16.2; Ont. 6.05(2) Commentary.

[5] N.S. C-16.4.

[6] N.B. 17-C.3; N.S. C-16.5; Ont. 6.05(2) Commentary.

[7] N.B. 17-C.4; N.S. C-16.6; Ont. 6.05(4).

[8] ABA-MC 9-101(A), (B); N.B. 17-C.5(a), (b); N.S. C-16.8; Ont. 3.05.10 Commentary.

[9] ABA-MR 1.11(c); N.B. 17-C.6; N.S. C-16.8; Ont. 6.05(5) Commentary.

[10] N.B. 17-C.9; N.S. C-16.9. In *Barreau de Montreal v. Claude Wagner* (1968), Q.B. 235 (Que. Q.B.) it was held that the respondent, then provincial Minister of Justice, was not subject to the disciplinary jurisdiction of the Bar in respect of a public speech in which he had criticized the conduct of a judge because he was then exercising his official or "Crown" functions. In *Gagnon v. Bar of Montreal* (1959), B.R. 92 (Que.) it was held that on the application for readmission to practice by a former judge, his conduct while in office might properly be considered by admissions authorities.

CHAPTER XI

FEES

RULE

The lawyer shall not:

(a) stipulate for, charge or accept any fee that is not fully disclosed, fair and reasonable;[1]

(b) appropriate any funds of the client held in trust or otherwise under the lawyer's control for or on account of fees without the express authority of the client, save as permitted by the rules of the governing body.[2]

Commentary

Factors to be Considered

1. A fair and reasonable fee will depend on and reflect such factors as:

(a) the time and effort required and spent;

(b) the difficulty and importance of the matter;

(c) whether special skill or service has been required and provided;

(d) the customary charges of other lawyers of equal standing in the locality in like matters and circumstances;

(e) in civil cases the amount involved, or the value of the subject matter;
(f) in criminal cases the exposure and risk to the client;
(g) the results obtained;
(h) tariffs or scales authorized by local law;
(i) such special circumstances as loss of other employment, urgency and uncertainty of reward;
(j) any relevant agreement between the lawyer and the client.[3]

A fee will not be fair and reasonable and may subject the lawyer to disciplinary proceedings if it is one that cannot be justified in the light of all pertinent circumstances, including the factors mentioned, or is so disproportionate to the services rendered as to introduce the element of fraud or dishonesty, or undue profit.[4]

2. It is in keeping with the best traditions of the legal profession to reduce or waive a fee in cases of hardship or poverty, or where the client or prospective client would otherwise effectively be deprived of legal advice or representation.[5]

Avoidance of Controversy

3. Breaches of this Rule and misunderstandings about fees and financial matters bring the legal profession into disrepute and reflect adversely upon the administration of justice. The lawyer should try to avoid controversy with the client over fees and should be ready to explain the basis for charges, especially if the client is unsophisticated or uninformed about the proper basis and measurements for fees. The lawyer should give the client an early and fair estimate of fees and disbursements, pointing out any uncertainties involved, so that the client may be able to make an informed decision. When something unusual or unforeseen occurs that may

substantially affect the amount of the fee, the lawyer should forestall misunderstandings or disputes by explaining this to the client.[6]

Interest on Overdue Accounts

4.   Save where permitted by law or local practice, the lawyer should not charge interest on an overdue account except by prior agreement with the client and then only at a reasonable rate.[7]

Apportionment and Division of Fees

5.   The lawyer who acts for two or more clients in the same matter is under a duty to apportion the fees and disbursements equitably among them in the absence of agreement otherwise.[8]

6.   A fee will not be a fair one within the meaning of the Rule if it is divided with another lawyer who is not a partner or associate unless (a) the client consents, either expressly or impliedly, to the employment of the other lawyer and (b) the fee is divided in proportion to the work done and responsibility assumed.[9]

Hidden Fees

7.   The fiduciary relationship that exists between lawyer and client requires full disclosure in all financial matters between them and prohibits the lawyer from accepting any hidden fees. No fee, reward, costs, commission, interest, rebate, agency or forwarding allowance or other compensation whatsoever related to the professional employment may be taken by the lawyer from anyone other than the client without full disclosure to and consent of the client. Where the lawyer's fees are being paid by someone other than the client, such as a legal aid agency, a borrower, or a personal representative, the

consent of such other person will be required. So far as disbursements are concerned, only *bona fide* and specified payments to others may be included. If the lawyer is financially interested in the person to whom the disbursements are made, such as an investigating, brokerage or copying agency, the lawyer shall expressly disclose this fact to the client.[10]

Sharing Fees with Non-Lawyers

8. Any arrangement whereby the lawyer directly or indirectly shares, splits or divides fees with notaries public, law students, clerks or other non-lawyers who bring or refer business to the lawyer's office is improper and constitutes professional misconduct. It is also improper for the lawyer to give any financial or other reward to such persons for referring business.[11]

9. The lawyer shall not enter into a lease or other arrangement whereby a landlord or other person directly or indirectly shares in the fees or revenues generated by the law practice.[12]

Contingent Fees

10. It is proper for the lawyer to enter into an arrangement with the client for a contingent fee, if the fee is fair and reasonable and the lawyer adheres to any legislation, rules of court or local practice relating to such an arrangement.[13]

---

[1] Alta. 13-S.O.P.; ABA-MC EC 2-17 to EC 2-19; ABA-MR DR 2-106; B.C. 9(1); N.B. 9-R(a); N.S. R-12; Ont. 2.08(1); Que. 3.08.01.

[2] N.B. 9-R(b); Ont. 2.08(12).

[3] Alta. 13-R.1; ABA-MC DR 2-106(B); ABA-MR 1.5(a); N.B. 9-C.2(a); N.S. R-12 Guiding Principles; Ont. 2.08 Commentary; Que. 3.08.02.

4 N.B. 9-C.2(b).

5 ABA-MC EC 2-16, 2-25; N.B. 9-C.1; N.S. C-12.2; Ont. 2.08 Commentary.

6 Alta. 13-R.2, R.4; ABA-MR 1.5(b); N.B. 9-C.3(a), (b); N.S. C-12.1; Ont. 2.08 Commentary; Que. 3.08.04, 3.08.05.

7 N.B. 9-4(a), (b); N.S. C-12.3; Ont. 2.08 Commentary; Que. 3.08.07.

8 N.B. 9-C.6; N.S. C-12.4; Ont. 2.08(7).

9 Alta. 13-R.7(b); ABA-MC DR 2-107(A); ABA-MR 1.5(e); N.B. 9-C.7(ii); N.S. C-12.5; Ont. 2.08(8).

10 B.C. 9(7) to 9(9); N.B. 9-C.9(a) to (c); N.S. C-12.6 to 12.8; Ont. 2.08 Commentary.

11 Alta. 13-R.7(c); B.C. 9(6); N.B. 9-C.8(i), (ii); N.S. C-12.9; Ont. 2.08(10); Que. 3.05.14.

12 ABA-MC EC 2-20, EC 5-7, DR 5-103(A)(2); N.B. 9-C.8(iii); N.S. C-12.10.

13 Alta. 13-R.3; ABA-MC EC 2-20; ABA-MR 1.5(c), (d)(2); N.B. 9-C.10; N.S. C-12.11; Ont. 2.08(3). For many years, Ontario was the only jurisdiction in North America in which contingent fees were prohibited. In 2002, as a result of the Ontario Court of Appeal's decision in *McIntyre Estate v. Ontario (Attorney General)* (2002), 61 O.R. (3d) 257, the Law Society of Upper Canada amended its *Rules of Professional Conduct* to allow lawyers to enter into contingent fee agreements except in family law or criminal or quasi-criminal matters: see Ont. 2.08 (3) – (5) and accompanying commentary.

CHAPTER XII

WITHDRAWAL

RULE

The lawyer owes a duty to the client not to withdraw services except for good cause and upon notice appropriate in the circumstances.[1]

Commentary

Guiding Principles

1. Although the client has a right to terminate the lawyer-client relationship at will, the lawyer does not enjoy the same freedom of action. Having once accepted professional employment the lawyer should complete the task as ably as possible unless there is justifiable cause for terminating the relationship.[2]

2. The lawyer who withdraws from employment should act so as to minimize expense and avoid prejudice to the client, doing everything reasonably possible to facilitate the expeditious and orderly transfer of the matter to the successor lawyer.[3]

3. Where withdrawal is required or permitted by this Rule the lawyer must comply with all applicable rules of court as well as local rules and practice.[4]

Obligatory Withdrawal

4.   In some circumstances the lawyer will be under a duty to withdraw. The obvious example is following discharge by the client. Other examples are:

(a) if the lawyer is instructed by the client to do something inconsistent with the lawyer's duty to the court or tribunal and, following explanation, the client persists in such instructions;

(b) if the client is guilty of dishonourable conduct in the proceedings or is taking a position solely to harass or maliciously injure another;

(c) if it becomes clear that the lawyer's continued employment will lead to a breach of these Rules such as, for example, a breach of the Rules relating to conflict of interest; or

(d) if it develops that the lawyer is not competent to handle the matter. In all these situations there is a duty to inform the client that the lawyer must withdraw.[5]

Optional Withdrawal

5.   Situations where a lawyer would be entitled to withdraw, although not under a positive duty to do so, will as a rule arise only where there has been a serious loss of confidence between lawyer and client. Such a loss of confidence goes to the very basis of the relationship. Thus, the lawyer who is deceived by the client will have justifiable cause for withdrawal. Again, the refusal of the client to accept and act upon the lawyer's advice on a significant point might indicate such a loss of confidence. At the same time, the lawyer should not use the threat of withdrawal as a device to force the client into making a hasty decision on a difficult question. The lawyer may withdraw if unable to obtain instructions from the client.[6]

Non-Payment of Fees

6. Failure on the part of the client after reasonable notice to provide funds on account of disbursements or fees will justify withdrawal by the lawyer unless serious prejudice to the client would result.[7]

Notice to Client

7. No hard and fast rules can be laid down as to what will constitute reasonable notice prior to withdrawal. Where the matter is covered by statutory provisions or rules of court, these will govern. In other situations the governing principle is that the lawyer should protect the client's interests so far as possible and should not desert the client at a critical stage of a matter or at a time when withdrawal would put the client in a position of disadvantage or peril.[8]

Duty Following Withdrawal

8. Upon discharge or withdrawal the lawyer should:

(a) deliver in an orderly and expeditious manner to or to the order of the client all papers and property to which the client is entitled;[9]
(b) give the client all information that may be required about the case or matter;
(c) account for all funds of the client on hand or previously dealt with and refund any remuneration not earned during the employment;[10]
(d) promptly render an account for outstanding fees and disbursements;[11]
(e) cooperate with the successor lawyer for the purposes outlined in paragraph.[12]

The obligation in clause (a) to deliver papers and property is

subject to the lawyer's right of lien referred to in paragraph 11.
In the event of conflicting claims to such papers and property,
the lawyer should make every effort to have the claimants
settle the dispute.[13]

9.   Cooperation with the successor lawyer will normally
include providing any memoranda of fact and law that have
been prepared by the lawyer in connection with the matter,
but confidential information not clearly related to the matter
should not be divulged without the express consent of the
client.[14]

10.   The lawyer acting for several clients in a case or matter
who ceases to act for one or more of them should cooperate
with the successor lawyer or lawyers to the extent permitted
by this Code, and should seek to avoid any unseemly rivalry,
whether real or apparent.[15]

Lien for Unpaid Fees

11.   Where upon the discharge or withdrawal of the lawyer the
question of a right of lien for unpaid fees and disbursements
arises, the lawyer should have due regard to the effect of its
enforcement upon the client's position. Generally speaking,
the lawyer should not enforce such a lien if the result would
be to prejudice materially the client's position in any
uncompleted matter.[16]

Duty of Successor Lawyer

12.   Before accepting employment, the successor lawyer
should be satisfied that the former lawyer approves, or has
withdrawn or been discharged by the client. It is quite proper
for the successor lawyer to urge the client to settle or take
reasonable steps toward settling or securing any account owed
to the former lawyer, especially if the latter withdrew for good

cause or was capriciously discharged. But if a trial or hearing is in progress or imminent, or if the client would otherwise be prejudiced, the existence of an outstanding account should not be allowed to interfere with the successor lawyer acting for the client.[17]

Dissolution of Law Firm

13. When a law firm is dissolved, this will usually result in the termination of the lawyer-client relationship as between a particular client and one or more of the lawyers involved. In such cases, most clients will prefer to retain the services of the lawyer whom they regarded as being in charge of their business prior to the dissolution. However, the final decision rests in each case with the client, and the lawyers who are no longer retained by the client should act in accordance with the principles here set out, and in particular commentary.[18]

---

1 Alta. 14-S.O.P.; ABA-MC EC 2-32, DR 2-110(A), (C); N.B. 10-R; N.S. R-11; Ont. 2.09(1); Que. 3.03.04. For cases, see 4 Can. Abr. (2d) under "Barristers and Solicitors: Termination of Relationship", paras. 101-02 and supplements.
2 N.B. 10-C.1(a); N.S. R-11 Guiding Principle 1; Ont. 2.09(1) Commentary.
3 ABA-MC EC 2-32, DR 2-110(A); N.B. 10-C.1(b)(i),(ii); N.S. R-11 Guiding Principle 2; Ont. 2.09(8). Provincial Rules of Court provide for the giving of notice of change of solicitors and for the bringing of motions for leave to withdraw. For cases, see 4 Can. Abr. (2d) under "Barristers and Solicitors: Change of Solicitors", paras. 342-58 and supplements. In legal aid cases, provincial regulations may also require notice to the plan administrators; see, e.g., in R.R.O. 1990, Reg. 710, s. 63(1)(a).
4 N.B. 10-C.1(b)(iii); N.S. R-11 Guiding Principle 3.
5 Alta. 14-R.1; ABA-MC DR 2-110(B); ABA-MR 1.16(a); B.C. 10(1); N.B. 10-C. 3; N.S. C-11.1, C-11.2; Ont. 2.09(7); Que. 3.02.09.
6 Alta. 14-R.2; ABA-MR 1.16(b); B.C. 10(2); N.B. 10-C.4(a); N.S. C-11.3 to C-11.5; Ont. 2.09(2); Que. 3.03.04, 3.03.05. Failure to instruct counsel constitutes repudiation which counsel could accept and terminate the employment.
7 B.C. 10(6), 10(7); N.B. 10-C.4(vi), 4(b); N.S. C-11.6; Ont. 2.09(3).
8 ABA-MC DR 2-110(A)(2); N.B. 10-C.2(b); N.S. C-11.7, 11.8; Ont. 2.09(1) Commentary.

9 B.C. 10(8)(d)(ii).

10 B.C. 10(8)(d)(i).

11 Alta. 14-R.4.

12 Alta. 14-R.3; B.C. 10(8)(e).

13 ABA-MC EC 2-32; ABA-MR 1.16(d); N.B. 10-C.5(a); N.S. C-11.9, 11.10; Ont. 2.09(9).

14 N.B. 10-C.5(a); N.S. C-11.11.

15 N.B. 10-C.5(b); N.S. C-11.12; Ont. 2.09(9) Commentary.

16 Alta. 13-R.9; N.B. 10-C.6; N.S. C-11.13; Ont. 2.09(9) Commentary.

17 Alta. 14-R.5; N.B. 10-C.7; N.S. C-1.14, 11.15; Ont. 2.09(10).

18 N.B. 10-C.8; N.S. C-11.16, 11.17; Ont. 2.09(7) Commentary.

CHAPTER XIII

THE LAWYER AND THE ADMINISTRATION OF JUSTICE

RULE

The lawyer should encourage public respect for and try to improve the administration of justice.[1]

Commentary

Guiding Principles

1. The admission to and continuance in the practice of law imply a basic commitment by the lawyer to the concept of equal justice for all within an open, ordered and impartial system. However, judicial institutions will not function effectively unless they command the respect of the public. Because of changes in human affairs and the imperfection of human institutions, constant efforts must be made to improve the administration of justice and thereby maintain public respect for it.[2]

2. The lawyer, by training, opportunity and experience, is in a position to observe the workings and discover the strengths and weaknesses of laws, legal institutions and public authorities. The lawyer should, therefore, lead in seeking improvements in the legal system, but any criticisms and proposals should be *bona fide* and reasoned.[3]

Scope of the Rule

3.   The obligation outlined in the Rule is not restricted to the lawyer's professional activities but is a general responsibility resulting from the lawyer's position in the community. The lawyer's responsibilities are greater than those of a private citizen. The lawyer must not subvert the law by counselling or assisting in activities that are in defiance of it and must do nothing to lessen the respect and confidence of the public in the legal system of which the lawyer is a part. The lawyer should take care not to weaken or destroy public confidence in legal institutions or authorities by broad irresponsible allegations of corruption or partiality. The lawyer in public life must be particularly careful in this regard because the mere fact of being a lawyer will lend weight and credibility to any public statements. For the same reason, the lawyer should not hesitate to speak out against an injustice. (As to test cases, see commentary 8 of the Rule relating to advising clients.)[4]

Criticism of the Tribunal

4.   Although proceedings and decisions of tribunals are properly subject to scrutiny and criticism by all members of the public, including lawyers, members of tribunals are often prohibited by law or custom from defending themselves. Their inability to do so imposes special responsibilities upon lawyers. Firstly, the lawyer should avoid criticism that is petty, intemperate or unsupported by a *bona fide* belief in its real merit, bearing in mind that in the eyes of the public, professional knowledge lends weight to the lawyer's judgements or criticism. Secondly, if the lawyer has been involved in the proceedings, there is the risk that any criticism may be, or may appear to be, partisan rather than objective. Thirdly, where a tribunal is the object of unjust criticism, the lawyer, as a participant in the administration of justice, is uniquely able to and should support the tribunal, both because

its members cannot defend themselves and because the lawyer is thereby contributing to greater public understanding of and therefore respect for the legal system.[5]

Improving the Administration of Justice

5. The lawyer who seeks legislative or administrative changes should disclose whose interest is being advanced, whether it be the lawyer's interest, that of a client, or the public interest. The lawyer may advocate such changes on behalf of a client without personally agreeing with them, but the lawyer who purports to act in the public interest should espouse only those changes that the lawyer conscientiously believes to be in the public interest.[6]

---

[1] Alta. 1-R.1 to R.3; ABA-MC Canon 8, DR 1-102 (A)(5); N.B. 20-R; N.S. R-21; Ont. 4.06(1); Que. 2.01 to 2.10.

[2] N.B. 20-C.2; N.S. R-21 Guiding Principle; Ont. 4.06(1) Commentary. Cf. the traditional barristers' oath: "...to protect and defend the right and interest of such of your fellow-citizens as may employ you.... You shall not pervert the law to favour or prejudice any man...". ABA-MC ECs 8-1, 8-2, 8-9: "Changes in human affairs and imperfections in human institutions make necessary constant efforts to maintain and improve our legal system. This system should function in a manner that commands public respect and fosters the use of legal remedies to achieve redress of grievances.... Rules of law are deficient if they are not just, understandable and responsive to the needs of society.... The advancement of our legal system is of vital importance in maintaining the rule of law and in facilitating orderly changes...".

[3] ABA-MC EC 8-1, 8-2, 8-9; N.B. 20-C.3(a); N.S. R-21 Guiding Principle; Ont. 4.06(1) Commentary. ABA-MC ECs 8-1, 8-2: "By reason of education and experience, lawyers are especially qualified to recognize deficiencies in the legal system and to initiate corrective measures therein.... [The lawyer] should encourage the simplification of laws and the repeal or amendment of laws that are outmoded. Likewise, legal procedures should be improved whenever experience indicates a change is needed."

[4] Alta. 1-R.5; N.S. C-21.1 to 21.4; Ont. 4.06(1).

[5] Alta. 1-C.2; ABA-MC EC 8-6; N.B. 20-C.4; N.S. C-21.5 to 21.8; Ont. 4.06(1) Commentary; Que. 2.01.

[6] Alta. 1-C.2; ABA-MC EC 8-4; N.B. 20-C.3(b), (c); N.S. C-21.9; Ont. 4.06(2) and Commentary.

CHAPTER XIV

ADVERTISING, SOLICITATION AND MAKING LEGAL SERVICES AVAILABLE

RULE

Lawyers should make legal services available to the public in an efficient and convenient manner that will command respect and confidence, and by means that are compatible with the integrity, independence and effectiveness of the profession.[1]

Commentary

Guiding Principles

1.   It is essential that a person requiring legal services be able to find a qualified lawyer with a minimum of difficulty or delay. In a relatively small community where lawyers are well known, the person will usually be able to make an informed choice and select a qualified lawyer in whom to have confidence. However, in larger centres these conditions will often not obtain. As the practice of law becomes increasingly complex and many individual lawyers restrict their activities to particular fields of law, the reputations of lawyers and their competence or qualification in particular fields may not be sufficiently well known to enable a person to make an informed choice. Thus one who has had little or no contact with lawyers or who is a stranger in the community may have difficulty finding a lawyer with the special skill required for a

particular task. Telephone directories, legal directories and referral services may help find a lawyer, but not necessarily the right one for the work involved. Advertising of legal services by the lawyer may assist members of the public and thereby result in increased access to the legal system. Where local rules permit, the lawyer may, therefore, advertise legal services to the general public.[2]

2.   When considering whether advertising in a particular area meets the public need, consideration must be given to the clientele to be served. For example, in a small community with a stable population a person requiring a lawyer for a particular purpose will not have the same difficulty in selecting one as someone in a newly established community or a large city. Thus the governing body must have freedom of action in determining the nature and content of advertising that will best meet the community need.

3.   Despite the lawyer's economic interest in earning a living, advertising must comply with any rules prescribed by the governing body, must be consistent with the public interest, and must not detract from the integrity, independence or effectiveness of the legal profession. Advertising must not mislead the uninformed or arouse unattainable hopes and expectations, and must not adversely affect the quality of legal services, or be so undignified or otherwise offensive as to be prejudicial to the interests of the public or the legal profession.[3]

Finding a Lawyer

4.   The lawyer who is consulted by a prospective client should be ready to assist in finding the right lawyer to deal with the problem. If unable to act, for example, because of lack of qualification in the particular field, the lawyer should assist in finding a practitioner who is qualified and able to act.

Such assistance should be given willingly and, except in very special circumstances, without charge.[4]

5. The lawyer may also assist in making legal services available by participating in legal aid plans and referral services, by engaging in programs of public information, education or advice concerning legal matters, and by being considerate of those who seek advice but are inexperienced in legal matters or cannot readily explain their problems.[5]

6. The lawyer has a general right to decline particular employment (except when assigned as counsel by a court) but it is a right the lawyer should be slow to exercise if the probable result would be to make it very difficult for a person to obtain legal advice or representation. Generally speaking, the lawyer should not exercise the right merely because the person seeking legal services or that person's cause is unpopular or notorious, or because powerful interests or allegations of misconduct or malfeasance are involved, or because of the lawyer's private opinion about the guilt of the accused. As stated in commentary 4, the lawyer who declines employment should assist the person to obtain the services of another lawyer competent in the particular field and able to act.[6]

7. Lawyers may offer professional services to prospective clients by any means except means:

(a) that are false or misleading;[7]
(b) that amount to coercion, duress, or harassment;
(c) that take advantage of a person who is vulnerable or who has suffered a traumatic experience and has not yet had a chance to recover;
(d) that are intended to influence a person who has retained another lawyer for a particular matter to change that person's lawyer for that matter, unless the

change is initiated by the person or the other lawyer;[8] or

(e) that otherwise bring the profession or the administration of justice into disrepute.[9]

Enforcement of Restrictive Rules

8. The lawyer should adhere to rules made by the governing body with respect to making legal services available and respecting advertising, but rigid adherence to restrictive rules should be enforced with discretion where the lawyer who may have infringed such rules acted in good faith in trying to make legal services available more efficiently, economically and conveniently than they would otherwise have been.

---

[1] Alta. 5-S.O.P.; ABA-MC Canon 2, EC 2-1; ABA-MR 7; B.C. 14(3); N.B. 16-R; N.S. R-15; Ont. 3.0.1.

[2] ABA-MC EC 2-6 to EC 2-8; ABA-MR 7.2; N.B. 16-C.1; N.S. R-15 Guiding Principle; Ont. 3.01 Commentary.

[3] Alta. 5-R.2, R.3; ABA-MC EC 2-9 to EC 2-14, DR 2-101(B); N.B. 16-C.3; Que. 5.02, 5.05.

[4] Alta. 5-R.1; N.S. C-15.1; Ont. 3.01 Commentary.

[5] ABA-MC EC 2-15, 2-16, DR 2-103; N.S. C-15.3; Ont. 3.01 Commentary.

[6] Alta. 5-R.1; ABA-MC EC 2-26 to EC 2-30; N.S. 15.4; Ont. 3.01 Commentary.

[7] N.B. 16-C.4(a).

[8] N.B. 16-C.4(d).

[9] Alta. 5-C.G.2.

CHAPTER XV

RESPONSIBILITY TO THE PROFESSION GENERALLY

RULE

The lawyer should assist in maintaining the integrity of the profession and should participate in its activities.[1]

Commentary

Guiding Principles

1. Unless the lawyer who tends to depart from standards of professional conduct is checked at an early stage, loss or damage to clients or others may ensue. Evidence of minor breaches may, on investigation, disclose a more serious situation or may indicate the beginning of a course of conduct that would lead to serious breaches in the future. It is, therefore, proper for a lawyer to report to a governing body any occurrence involving a breach of this Code unless the information is privileged or it would otherwise be unlawful for the lawyer to do so. Where, however, there is a reasonable likelihood that someone will suffer serious damage as a consequence of an apparent breach, for example, where a shortage of trust funds is involved, the lawyer has an obligation to the profession to report the matter unless the information is privileged or it is otherwise unlawful to do so.[2] The lawyer also has an obligation to the profession to report to

the governing body (unless to do so would be unlawful or would involve a breach of privilege):

    (a)   a misappropriation or misapplication of trust money or other property held in trust;[3]

    (b)   the abandonment of a law practice;

    (c)   participation in criminal activity related to a lawyer's practice;

    (d)   the mental instability of a lawyer of such a serious nature that the lawyer's clients are likely to be severely prejudiced; and

    (e)   any other situation where a lawyer's client is likely to be severely prejudiced.[4]

In all cases, the report must be made *bona fide* and without ulterior motive. Further, subject to local rules, the lawyer must not act on a client's instructions to recover from another lawyer money or other property allegedly misappropriated by the other lawyer unless the client authorizes disclosure to the governing body and the lawyer makes such disclosure.

2.   The lawyer has a duty to reply promptly to any communication from the governing body.[5]

3.   The lawyer should not in the course of a professional practice write letters, whether to a client, another lawyer or any other person, that are abusive, offensive or otherwise totally inconsistent with the proper tone of a professional communication from a lawyer.[6]

Participation in Professional Activities

4.   In order that the profession may discharge its public responsibility of providing independent and competent legal services, the individual lawyer should do everything possible to assist the profession to function properly and effectively. In

this regard, participation in such activities as law reform, continuing legal education, tutorials, legal aid programs, community legal services, professional conduct and discipline, liaison with other professions and other activities of the governing body or local, provincial or national associations, although often time-consuming and without tangible reward, is essential to the maintenance of a strong, independent and useful profession.[7]

---

[1] ABA-MC Canon 1, EC 1-4; ABA-MR 8; Alta. 3-S.O.P., 3-R.1; N.B. 19-R(a); N.S. R-18.

[2] ABA-MC EC 1-2, 1-4, DR 1-103; ABA-MR 8.3; B.C. 13(1), (2); N.B. 15-C.6; N.S. C-18.1, 18.2; *Law Society of Prince Edward Island v. Aylward* [2001] L.S.D.D. No. 48.

[3] B.C. 13(1)(b).

[4] Alta. 3-R.4; Que. 4.02.01.

[5] Alta. 3-R.3; B.C. 13(3); N.B. 19-C.1; N.S. C-18.4; Que. 4.03.02.

[6] Alta. 3-R.2; N.B. 19-C.2.

[7] ABA-MC EC 6-2, 8-1, 8-2, 8-9, 9-6; Alta. 3-C.G.1; N.B. 19-C.3; N.S. C-18.5; Que. 4.04.01.

CHAPTER XVI

RESPONSIBILITY TO LAWYERS AND OTHERS

RULE

The lawyer's conduct toward all persons with whom the lawyer comes into contact in practice should be characterized by courtesy and good faith.[1]

Commentary

Guiding Principles

1. Public interest demands that matters entrusted to the lawyer be dealt with effectively and expeditiously. Fair and courteous dealing on the part of each lawyer engaged in a matter will contribute materially to this end. The lawyer who behaves otherwise does a disservice to the client, and neglect of the Rule will impair the ability of lawyers to perform their function properly.[2]

2. Any ill feeling that may exist or be engendered between clients, particularly during litigation, should never be allowed to influence lawyers in their conduct and demeanour toward each other or the parties. The presence of personal animosity between lawyers involved in a matter may cause their judgment to be clouded by emotional factors and hinder the proper resolution of the matter. Personal remarks or references

between them should be avoided. Haranguing or offensive tactics interfere with the orderly administration of justice and have no place in our legal system.[3]

3.   The lawyer should accede to reasonable requests for trial dates, adjournments, waivers of procedural formalities and similar matters that do not prejudice the rights of the client. The lawyer who knows that another lawyer has been consulted in a matter should not proceed by default in the matter without enquiry and warning.[4]

Avoidance of Sharp Practices

4.   The lawyer should avoid sharp practice and not take advantage of or act without fair warning upon slips, irregularities or mistakes on the part of other lawyers not going to the merits or involving any sacrifice of the client's rights. The lawyer should not, unless required by the transaction, impose on other lawyers impossible, impractical or manifestly unfair conditions of trust, including those with respect to time restraints and the payment of penalty interest.[5]

5.   The lawyer should not use a tape-recorder or other device to record a conversation, whether with a client, another lawyer or anyone else, even if lawful, without first informing the other person of the intention to do so.[6]

6.   The lawyer should answer with reasonable promptness all professional letters and communications from other lawyers that require an answer and should be punctual in fulfilling all commitments.[7]

Undertakings

7.   The lawyer should give no undertaking that cannot be fulfilled, should fulfill every undertaking given, and should

scrupulously honour any trust condition once accepted.[8] Undertakings and trust conditions should be written or confirmed in writing and should be absolutely unambiguous in their terms. If the lawyer giving an undertaking does not intend to accept personal responsibility, this should be stated clearly in the undertaking itself. In the absence of such a statement, the person to whom the undertaking is given is entitled to expect that the lawyer giving it will honour it personally. If the lawyer is unable or unwilling to honour a trust condition imposed by someone else, the subject of the trust condition should be immediately returned to the person imposing the trust condition unless its terms can be forthwith amended in writing on a mutually agreeable basis.[9]

8.   The lawyer should not communicate upon or attempt to negotiate or compromise a matter directly with any party who is represented by a lawyer except through or with the consent of that lawyer.[10]

Acting Against Another Lawyer

9.   The lawyer should avoid ill-considered or uninformed criticism of the competence, conduct, advice or charges of other lawyers, but should be prepared, when requested, to advise and represent a client in a complaint involving another lawyer.[11]

10.   The same courtesy and good faith should characterize the lawyer's conduct toward lay persons lawfully representing others or themselves.[12]

11.   The lawyer who is retained by another lawyer as counsel or adviser in a particular matter should act only as counsel or adviser and respect the relationship between the other lawyer and the client.[13]

---

[1] ABA-MC EC 7-36 to 7-38, DR 7-101(A)(1); ABA-MR 3.4; Alta. 3-R.1, 4-S.O.P.; B.C. 1(4), 11; N.B. 15-R; N.S. R-13; Ont. 6.03(1); Que. 4.03.03.

[2] Ont. 6.03(1) Commentary; N.S. R-13 Guiding Principle. In Ontario, The Advocates' Society has published *Principles of Civility for Advocates* as an educational tool for the encouragement and maintenance of civility in our justice system. See Appendix.

[3] ABA-MC EC 7-37; N.S. C-13.1; Ont. 6.03(1) Commentary; M.M. Orkin, *Legal Ethics: A Study of Professional Conduct* (Toronto: Cartwright & Jane, 1957) at pp.131-32; N.B. D-4: "...it is the duty of counsel to 'try the merits of the cause and not to try each other'."

[4] ABA-MC EC 7-38, 7-39; Alta 4-R.4; N.B. 15-C.2(i), (iii); N.S. C-13.3; Ont. 6.03(2).

[5] Alta 1-R.1; N.B. 15-C.4; N.S. C-13.2; Ont. 6.03(3).

[6] Alta. 1-R.7; B.C. 11(14); N.B. 15-C.2(iv); N.S. C-13.4; Ont. 6.03(4). "[T]o build up a client's case on the slips of an opponent is not the duty of a professional man.... Solicitors do not do their duty to their clients by insisting upon the strict letter of their rights. That is the sort of thing which, if permitted, brings the administration of justice into odium," per Middleton J. in *Re Arthur and Town of Meaford* (1915), 34 O.L.R. 231 at 233-34 (Ont. H.C.).

[7] Alta. 1-R.5; B.C. 11(6); N.B. 15-C.2(v); N.S. C-13.5; Ont. 6.03(6).

[8] Alta. 1-R.10.

[9] Alta. 1-R.11; B.C. 11(7); N.B. 15-C.3; Ont. 6.03(8); N.S. C-13.6 to C-13.9.

10 ABA-MC EC 7-18; Alta. 1-R.6; B.C. 4(1.1); N.B. 15-C.2(ii); N.S. C-13.10; Ont. 6.03(7).

11 ABA-MC EC 2-28; B.C. 11(13); N.B. 15-C.5; N.S. C-13.12; Ont. 6.03(1) Commentary.

12 N.B. 15-C.2(vii); N.S. C-13.11.

13 N.B. 15-C.2(vi); N.S. C-13.11.

CHAPTER XVII

PRACTICE BY
UNAUTHORIZED PERSONS

RULE

The lawyer should assist in preventing the unauthorized practice of law.[1]

Commentary

Guiding Principles

1.   Statutory provisions against the practice of law by unauthorized persons are for the protection of the public. Unauthorized persons may have technical or personal ability, but they are immune from control, regulation and, in the case of misconduct, from discipline by any governing body. Their competence and integrity have not been vouched for by an independent body representative of the legal profession. Moreover, the client of a lawyer who is authorized to practise has the protection and benefit of the solicitor-client privilege, the lawyer's duty of secrecy, the professional standards of care that the law requires of lawyers, as well as the authority that the courts exercise over them. Other safeguards include group professional liability insurance, rights with respect to the taxation of bills, rules respecting trust monies, and requirements for the maintenance of compensation funds.[2]

Suspended or Disbarred Persons

2.   The lawyer should not, without the approval of the governing body, employ in any capacity having to do with the practice of law (a) a lawyer who is under suspension as a result of disciplinary proceedings, or (b) a person who has been disbarred as a lawyer or has been permitted to resign while facing disciplinary proceedings and has not been reinstated.[3]

Supervision of Employees

3.   The lawyer must assume complete professional responsibility for all business entrusted to the lawyer, maintaining direct supervision over staff and assistants such as students, clerks and legal assistants to whom particular tasks and functions may be delegated. The lawyer who practises alone or operates a branch or part-time office should ensure that all matters requiring a lawyer's professional skill and judgment are dealt with by a lawyer qualified to do the work and that legal advice is not given by unauthorized persons, whether in the lawyer's name or otherwise. Furthermore, the lawyer should approve the amount of any fee to be charged to a client.[4]

Legal Assistants

4.   There are many tasks that can be performed by a legal assistant working under the supervision of a lawyer. It is in the interests of the profession and the public for the delivery of more efficient, comprehensive and better quality legal services that the training and employment of legal assistants be encouraged.[5]

5.   Subject to general and specific restrictions that may be established by local rules and practice, a legal assistant may perform any task delegated and supervised by a lawyer so long

as the lawyer maintains a direct relationship with the client and assumes full professional responsibility for the work. Legal assistants shall not perform any of the duties that lawyers only may perform or do things that lawyers themselves may not do. Generally speaking, the question of what the lawyer may delegate to a legal assistant turns on the distinction between the special knowledge of the legal assistant and the professional legal judgment of the lawyer, which must be exercised whenever it is required.[6]

6. A legal assistant should be permitted to act only under the supervision of a lawyer. Adequacy of supervision will depend on the type of legal matter, including the degree of standardization and repetitiveness of the matter as well as the experience of the legal assistant, both generally and with regard to the particular matter. The burden rests on the lawyer who employs a legal assistant to educate the latter about the duties to which the legal assistant may be assigned and also to supervise on a continuing basis the way in which the legal assistant carries them out so that the work of the legal assistant will be shaped by the lawyer's judgment.[7]

---

[1] ABA-MC Canon 3, DR 3-101(A), (B); ABA-MR 5.5; B.C. 12; N.B. 19-R(b); Ont. 6.07(1); N.S. R-19.

[2] ABA-MC EC 3-1, 3-3, 3-4; N.S. C-19.1; Ont. 6.07(1) Commentary. Cases and statutes provide that certain acts amount to "the practice of law"; see, for example:
B.C.: *Legal Profession Act*, R.S.B.C. 1998, c. 9, s. 1(1).
Man.: *Legal Profession Act*, C.C.S.M. c. L-107, s. 20(3).
Nfld.: *Law Society Act*, S.N.L. 1999, c. L-9.1, s. 2(2).
N.S.: *Barristers and Solicitors Act*, R.S.N.S. 1989, c. 30, s. 5(2).
N.W.T.: *Legal Profession Act*, R.S.N.W.T. 1988, c. L-2, s. 1.
P.E.I.: *Legal Profession Act*, R.S.P.E.I., 1988, c. L-6.1, s. 1(j).
Que.: *An Act respecting the Barreau du Québec*, R.S.Q. c.B-1, s. 128.
The statutes of all provinces prohibit the practice of law by unauthorized persons:
Alta.: *Legal Profession Act*, R.S.A. 2000, c. L-8, s. 106(1).
B.C.: *supra*, s. 15.
Man.: *supra*, s. 20(2).

Nfld.: *supra*, s. 76(1).
N.S.: *supra*, s. 5(1).
Ont.: *Law Society Act*, R.S.O. 1990, c. L8, s. 50(1), (2).
Que.: *supra*, ss. 132 et seq.
Sask.: *Legal Profession Act*, R.S.S., c. L-10, s. 5.
"To protect the public against persons who...set themselves up as competent to perform services that imperatively require the training and learning of a solicitor, although such persons are without either learning or experience to qualify them, is an urgent public service," per Robertson C.J.O. in *Rex ex rel. Smith v. Ott* (1950), O.R. 493 at 496 (Ont. C.A.). "When a man says in effect, I am not a lawyer but I will do the work of a lawyer for you he is offering his services as a lawyer. In offering his services as a lawyer he is holding himself out as a lawyer even though he makes it clear he is not a properly qualified lawyer," per Miller C.C.J. in *Regina v. Woods* (1962), O.W.N. 27 at 30.
3 N.B. 19-C.4; N.S. C-19.2; Ont. 6.07(2).
4 ABA-MC EC 3-5, 3-6; Alta. 2-R.4, 2-C.4.1; B.C. 12(1), 12(2); N.B. 19-C.5; N.S. C-19.3 to C-19.5.
5 B.C. 12(4), 12(8).
6 B.C. 12(5), 12(5.1), 12(6); N.B. 19-C.6; N.S. C-19.6.
7 ABA-MR 5.3; B.C. 12(7); N.S. C-19.7.

CHAPTER XVIII

PUBLIC APPEARANCES AND PUBLIC STATEMENTS BY LAWYERS

RULE

The lawyer who engages in public appearances and public statements should do so in conformity with the principles of the Code.[1]

Commentary

Guiding Principles

1. The lawyer who makes public appearances and public statements should behave in the same way as when dealing with clients, fellow practitioners and the courts. Dealings with the media are simply an extension of the lawyer's conduct in a professional capacity. The fact that an appearance is outside a courtroom or law office does not excuse conduct that would be considered improper in those contexts.[2]

Public Statements Concerning Clients

2. The lawyer's duty to the client demands that before making a public statement concerning the client's affairs, the lawyer must first be satisfied that any communication is in the best interests of the client and within the scope of the retainer. The lawyer owes a duty to the client to be qualified to

represent the client effectively before the public and not to
permit any personal interest or other cause to conflict with the
client's interests.[3]

3. When acting as an advocate, the lawyer should refrain
from expressing personal opinions about the merits of the
client's case.[4]

Standard of Conduct

4. The lawyer should, where possible, encourage public
respect for and try to improve the administration of justice. In
particular, the lawyer should treat fellow practitioners, the
courts and tribunals with respect, integrity and courtesy.
Lawyers are subject to a separate and higher standard of
conduct than that which might incur the sanction of the
court.[5]

5. The lawyer who makes public appearances and public
statements must comply with the requirements of
commentary 3 of the Rule in Chapter XIV relating to
advertising, solicitation and making legal services available.

Contacts with the Media

6. The media have recently shown greater interest in legal
matters than they did formerly. This is reflected in more
coverage of the passage of legislation at national and provincial
levels, as well as of cases before the courts and tribunal that
may have social, economic or political significance. This
interest has been heightened by the enactment of the *Canadian
Charter of Rights and Freedoms*. As a result, media reporters
regularly seek out the views not only of lawyers directly
involved in particular court and tribunal proceedings but also
of lawyers who represent special interest groups or have
recognized expertise in a given field in order to obtain

information or provide commentary.[6]

7.   Where the lawyer, by reason of professional involvement or otherwise, is able to assist the media in conveying accurate information to the public, it is proper for the lawyer to do so, provided that there is no infringement of the lawyer's obligations to the client, the profession, the courts and tribunals or the administration of justice, and provided also that the lawyer's comments are made *bona fide* and without malice or ulterior motive.[7]

8.   The lawyer may make contact with the media in a non-legal setting to publicize such things as fund-raising, expansion of hospitals or universities, promoting public institutions or political organizations, or speaking on behalf of organizations that represent various racial, religious or other special interest groups. This is a well established and completely proper role for the lawyer to play in view of the obvious contribution it makes to the community.[8]

9.   The lawyer is often called upon to comment publicly on the effectiveness of existing statutory or legal remedies, on the effect of particular legislation or decided cases, or to offer an opinion on causes that have been or are about to be instituted. It is permissible to do this in order to assist the public to understand the legal issues involved.[9]

10. The lawyer may also be involved as an advocate for special interest groups whose objective is to bring about changes in legislation, government policy or even a heightened public awareness about certain issues, and the lawyer may properly comment publicly about such changes.[10]

11. Given the variety of cases that can arise in the legal system, whether in civil, criminal or administrative matters, it is not feasible to set down guidelines that would anticipate every

possible situation. In some circumstances, the lawyer should
have no contact at all with the media; in others, there may be a
positive duty to contact the media in order to serve the client
properly. The latter situation will arise more often when
dealing with administrative boards and tribunals that are
instruments of government policy and hence susceptible to
public opinion.[11]

12. The lawyer should bear in mind when making a public
appearance or giving a statement that ordinarily the lawyer will
have no control over any editing that may follow, or the
context in which the appearance or statement may be used.[12]

13. This Rule should not be construed in such a way as to
discourage constructive comment or criticism.

---

[1] ABA-MR 3.6; N.B. 18-R; N.S. R-22.

[2] N.B. 18-C.1; N.S. R-22 Guiding Principle; Ont. 6.06(1) Commentary.

[3] B.C. 14(6.1); N.B. 18-C.2(a), (b); N.S. C-22.1; Ont. 6.06(1) Commentary.

[4] B.C. 14(6)(a).

[5] N.S. C-22.3; Que. 2.00.01.

[6] N.S. C-22.5.

[7] N.B. 18-C.3; N.S. C-22.6.

[8] N.B. 18-C.5; N.S. C-22.7; Ont. 6.06(1) Commentary.

[9] N.B. 18-C.4(a); Ont. 6.06(1) Commentary.

[10] N.B. 18-C.4(b); N.S. C-22.4; Ont. 6.06(1) Commentary.

[11] Ont. 6.06(1) Commentary; N.S. C-22.10.

[12] N.B. 18-C.7; N.S. C-22.13; Ont. 6.06(1) Commentary.

CHAPTER XIX

AVOIDING QUESTIONABLE CONDUCT

RULE

The lawyer should observe the rules of professional conduct set out in the Code in the spirit as well as in the letter.[1]

Commentary

Guiding Principles

1.   Public confidence in the administration of justice and the legal profession may be eroded by irresponsible conduct on the part of the individual lawyer. For that reason, even the appearance of impropriety should be avoided.[2]

2.   Our justice system is designed to try issues in an impartial manner and decide them upon the merits. Statements or suggestions that the lawyer could or would try to circumvent the system should be avoided because they might bring the lawyer, the legal profession and the administration of justice into disrepute.[3]

Duty after Leaving Public Employment

3.   After leaving public employment, the lawyer should not accept employment in connection with any matter in which

the lawyer had substantial responsibility or confidential information prior to leaving because to do so would give the appearance of impropriety even if none existed. However, it would not be improper for the lawyer to act professionally in such a matter on behalf of the particular public body or authority by which the lawyer had formerly been employed. As to confidential government information acquired when the lawyer was a public officer or employee, see commentary 14 of the Rule relating to confidential information.[4]

Retired Judges

4.   A judge who returns to practice after retiring or resigning from the bench should not (without the approval of the governing body) appear as a lawyer before the court of which the former judge was a member or before courts of inferior jurisdiction thereto in the province where the judge exercised judicial functions. If in a given case the former judge should be in a preferred position by reason of having held judicial office, the administration of justice would suffer; if the reverse were true, the client might suffer. There may, however, be cases where a governing body would consider that no preference or appearance of preference would result, for example, where the judge resigned for good reason after only a very short time on the bench. In this paragraph "judge" refers to one who was appointed as such under provincial legislation or section 96 of the *Constitution Act, 1867* and "courts" include chambers and administrative boards and tribunals.[5]

5.   Conversely, although it may be unavoidable in some circumstances or areas, generally speaking the lawyer should not appear before a judge if by reason of relationship or past association, the lawyer would appear to be in a preferred position.[6]

Inserting Retainer in Client's Will

6. Without express instructions from the client, it is improper for the lawyer to insert in the client's will a clause directing the executor to retain the lawyer's services in the administration of the estate.[7]

Duty to Meet Financial Obligations

7. The lawyer has a professional duty, quite apart from any legal liability, to meet financial obligations incurred or assumed in the course of practice when called upon to do so. Examples are agency accounts, obligations to members of the profession, fees or charges of witnesses, sheriffs, special examiners, registrars, reporters and public officials, as well as the deductible under a governing body's errors and omissions insurance policy.[8]

Dealings with Unrepresented Persons

8. The lawyer should not undertake to advise an unrepresented person but should urge such a person to obtain independent legal advice and, if the unrepresented person does not do so, the lawyer must take care to see that such person is not proceeding under the impression that the lawyer is protecting such person's interests. If the unrepresented person requests the lawyer to advise or act in the matter, the lawyer should be governed by the considerations outlined in the Rule relating to impartiality and conflict of interest between clients. The lawyer may have an obligation to a person whom the lawyer does not represent, whether or not such person is represented by a lawyer.[9]

Bail

9. The lawyer shall not stand bail for an accused person for

whom the lawyer or a partner or associate is acting, except where there is a family relationship with the accused, in which case the person should not be represented by the lawyer but may be represented by a partner or associate.

Standard of Conduct

10. The lawyer should try at all times to observe a standard of conduct that reflects credit on the legal profession and the administration of justice generally and inspires the confidence, respect and trust of both clients and the community.[10]

---

[1] ABA-MC Canon 9; ABA-MR 8.4; Alta. 1-R.1; N.B. 23-R(a); N.S. R-23; Que. 1.00.01. Cf. dictum of Hewart L.C.J. in *The King v. Sussex Justices* (1924), 1 K.B. 256 at 259 (K.B.D.): "[It] is of fundamental importance that justice should not only be done, but should manifestly and undoubtedly be seen to be done."
[2] ABA-MC EC 9-1, DR 9-101; N.B. 23-C.1; N.S. C-23.1.
[3] ABA-MC EC 9-4; N.B. 23-C.2; N.S. C-23.2.
[4] ABA-MC EC 9-3, DR 9-101(B); N.S. C-16.10.
[5] Ont. 6.08(4); N.S. C-16.11.
[6] Alta. 10-R.9.
[7] N.S. C-7.3.
[8] Alta. 8-R.2, R.3; B.C. 2(2); N.B. 23-C.4; Ont. 6.01(2); N.S. C-18.7.
[9] ABA-MR 4.3; Alta. 11-R.5; B.C. 4(1); Ont. 2.04(14); N.S. C-4.20.
[10] Alta. 15-R.2.

CHAPTER XX

NON-DISCRIMINATION

RULE

The lawyer shall respect the requirements of human rights and constitutional laws in force in Canada, and in its provinces and territories. Except where differential treatment is permitted by law, the lawyer shall not discriminate with respect to partnership or professional employment of other lawyers, articled students or any other person, or in professional dealings with other members of the profession or any other person on grounds including, but not limited to, an individual's ancestry, colour, perceived race, nationality, national origin, ethnic background or origin, language, religion, creed or religious belief, religious association or activities, age, sex, gender, physical characteristics, pregnancy, sexual orientation, marital or family status, source of income, political belief, association or activity, or physical or mental disability.[1]

Commentary

Duty of Non-Discrimination

1. The lawyer has a duty to respect the dignity and worth of all persons and to treat persons equally, without discrimination. Discrimination is defined as any distinction that disproportionately and negatively impacts on an individual

or group identifiable by the grounds listed in the Rule, in a way that it does not impact on others. This duty includes, but is not limited to:

(a) the requirement that the lawyer does not deny services or provide inferior services on the basis of the grounds noted in the Rule;[2]

(b) the requirement that the lawyer not discriminate against another lawyer in any professional dealings;

(c) the requirement that the lawyer act in accordance with the legal duty to accommodate and not engage in discriminatory employment practices; and

(d) the requirement that the lawyer prohibit partners, co-workers and employees and agents subject to the lawyer's direction and control from engaging in discriminatory practices.[3]

Extent of Duty of Non-Discrimination

2.   Failure by the lawyer to take reasonable steps to prevent or stop discrimination by the lawyer's partner, co-worker or by any employee or agent also violates the duty of non-discrimination.

Special Programs

3.   Discrimination does not include special programs designed to relieve disadvantage for individuals or groups on the grounds noted in the Rule.[4]

Responsibility

4.   Discriminatory attitudes on the part of partners, employees, agents or clients do not diminish the responsibility of the lawyer to refrain from discrimination in the provision of service or employment.

Discrimination in Employment

5.   The Rule applies to discrimination by lawyers in any
aspect of employment and working conditions, including
recruitment, hiring, promotion, training, allocation of work,
compensation, benefits, dismissal, lay-offs, discipline,
performance appraisal, and hours of work.[5]

It applies to all discrimination with repercussions for
employment and workplace conditions, including physical
work sites, washrooms, conferences, business travel and social
events. Examples of discrimination in employment include:

(a) setting unnecessary or unfair hiring criteria that tend
     to exclude applicants on prohibited grounds;
(b) asking questions during an employment or promotion
     interview that are not logically related to the essential
     requirements of the job;
(c) assigning work on the basis of factors or assumptions
     other than individual ability or denying work to
     lawyers on the basis of prohibited grounds;
(d) failing to provide appropriate maternity and parental
     leave thereby discriminating on the basis of sex or
     family status;
(e) failing to accommodate religious holidays or religious
     practices thereby discriminating on the basis of
     religion;
(f) requiring billable hour targets or workload
     expectations which effectively exclude those who have
     child care responsibilities and adversely affect such
     persons on the basis of family status or sex.

It is not considered discrimination when distinctions are made
as a result of a reasonable and *bona fide* occupational
qualification or requirement.[6] For example, if an applicant for
a position is not sufficiently proficient in the language(s)

required for the competent performance of the essential duties and responsibilities required in that position, it would not constitute discrimination to deny the applicant employment solely on the ground of language. Where facility in a particular language is clearly an essential requirement for the position, the employer is not prevented from demanding the necessary proficiency.

Duty of Accommodation

6.   One aspect of the duty of non-discrimination is the duty to accommodate the diverse needs of lawyers on the basis of grounds noted in the Rule. Such accommodation is required unless it would cause undue hardship to the lawyer. Examples of this type of accommodation include:

(a)   the provision of flexible hours to accommodate family responsibilities or to accommodate transportation difficulties for persons with disabilities;

(b)   the modification of the physical workplace to include wheelchair access, modified furniture and assistive devices;

(c)   a benefits policy that includes same sex couples;

(d)   adjusting the billable hour or workload expectations to accommodate family responsibilities;

(e)   accommodation of religious holidays or religious practices.

Sexual Harassment and Harassment

7.   Sexual harassment and harassment are forms of discrimination. Harassment includes any improper, abusive or unwelcome conduct that offends, embarrasses, humiliates, or degrades another person. The lawyer should in all areas of professional conduct refrain from engaging in vexatious comments or conduct that is known or reasonably ought to be

known to constitute sexual harassment or harassment.[7]

(a) Sexual harassment includes the use of a position of power to import sexual requirements into the workplace thereby negatively altering the working conditions of employees. Types of behaviour that constitute sexual harassment include, but are not limited to:

(i)   making sexist jokes causing embarrassment or offence, or that are by their nature clearly embarrassing or offensive;

(ii) leering;

(iii) displaying sexually offensive material;

(iv) using sexually degrading words to describe a person;

(v)   making derogatory or degrading remarks directed towards members of one sex or one's sexual orientation;

(vi) making sexually suggestive or obscene comments or gestures;

(vii) making unwelcome inquiries or comments about a person's sex life;

(viii) making unwelcome sexual flirtations, advances, or propositions;

(ix) engaging in persistent unwanted contact or attention after the end of a consensual relationship;

(x)   requests for sexual favours;

(xi) unwanted touching;

(xii) verbal abuse or threats; and

(xiii) sexual assault.

Sexual harassment can occur in the form of behaviour by a man towards a woman, between men, between women, or by a woman towards a man.[8]

(b) Harassment includes all conduct that erodes the dignity and equality of opportunity of the victim, particularly based on any of the grounds noted in the Rule. Types of behaviour that constitute harassment include, but are not limited to:

   (i) unwelcome remarks, jokes, comments, slurs, innuendoes or taunting about a person's body, attire, ancestry, colour, perceived race, nationality, national origin, ethnic background or origin, language, religion, creed or religious belief, religious association or activities, age, sex, gender, physical characteristics, pregnancy, sexual orientation, marital or family status, source of income, political belief, association or activity, physical or mental disability, or on other grounds;

   (ii) displaying or distributing racist, pornographic and other offensive material, calendars, posters, cartoons or drawings;

   (iii) practical jokes based on race, sex, or other prohibited grounds;

   (iv) unwelcome invitations or requests, particularly based on intimidation;

   (v) verbal abuse or threats;

   (vi) inappropriate or offensive gestures;

   (vii) physical assault;

   (viii) name calling; and

   (ix) condescension which undermines self-respect.

Discriminatory Activities

8. The lawyer must refrain from participating in discriminatory activities in his or her professional life.

[1] ABA-MR 8.4; Alta. 1-R.8, C.8; B.C. 2(3); N.B. 21-R; N.S. R-24; Ont. 5.04(1).

[2] N.S. C-24.1.

[3] N.B. 21-C.1.

[4] B.C. 2(6); N.B. 21-C.3(c); N.S. C-24.6.

[5] Alta. 1-C.8; N.B. 21-C.2(a); N.S. C-24.2; Ont. 5.04(3).

[6] N.B. 21-C.3(a)(i); N.S. C-24.4(a).

[7] Alta. 1-R.9, C.9; B.C. 2(5); N.B. 22-C.1, C.2(a); Ont. 5.03(1); Que. 4.02.01(y).

[8] N.B. 22-C.2(c); Ont. 5.03(1) Commentary.

CHAPTER XXI

THE LAWYER AS MEDIATOR

RULE

1. A lawyer who acts as a mediator shall, at the outset of the mediation, ensure that the parties to it understand fully that:

(a) the lawyer is not acting as a lawyer for either party but, as mediator, is acting to assist the parties to resolve the matters in issue, and

(b) although communications pertaining to and arising out of the mediation process may be covered by some other common law, civil law principles, statutory or other privilege or rule, they will not be covered by the solicitor-client privilege.[1]

2. A lawyer shall not act as a mediator if the lawyer or the lawyer's firm has acted or is acting in a matter that may reasonably be expected to become an issue during the mediation, except with the informed consent of all parties.[2]

Commentary

1. Generally, lawyers who serve as mediators are governed by the provisions of this Code except to the extent that those provisions are varied by this Chapter.[3]

2. Generally, lawyers who serve as mediators should suggest

and encourage the parties to seek the advice of separate counsel before and during the mediation process if they have not already done so. Where a lawyer who serves as a mediator prepares a draft contract for the consideration by the parties, the lawyer should advise and encourage them to seek separate independent legal representation concerning the draft.

---

[1] ABA-MC EC 5-20; Alta. 6-C.1.2; N.B. 13-C.2; Ont. 4.0.7.

[2] Ont. 4.07 Commentary.

[3] Alta. 15-C.G.2; Ont. 4.07 Commentary.

CHAPTER XXII

INDEPENDENCE OF THE BAR

RULE

1. The lawyer must exercise independent professional judgment in providing legal advice, services and representation to a client.[1]

2. The lawyer must conduct himself or herself in a manner that respects, protects and advances the independence of the bar.

Commentary

1. Independence is one of the foundational values of the legal profession. A lawyer must exercise independent judgment and at all times act in the best interests of the client. Many of the professional duties set forth in other chapters of this Code may be seen as aspects of the independence of the bar, including the duty to discharge all duties owed to clients and others with integrity (Chapter I), the duty to be both honest and candid when advising clients (Chapter III), the duty to hold in strict confidence all information concerning the business and affairs of the client acquired in the course of the professional relationship (Chapter IV), the duty not to act or to continue to act in a matter when there is or is likely to be a conflicting interest (Chapter V), the duty not to act for a client where the lawyer's duty to the client and the personal interests of the lawyer are in conflict (Chapter VI), and the duty to

represent the client resolutely and fearlessly (Chapter IX).

2. In the legal profession the right of self-governance is at the heart of the independence of the bar. The importance of the legal profession remaining independent from government control was emphasized in a unanimous 1982 judgment of the Supreme Court of Canada:

> *The independence of the bar from the State in all its pervasive manifestations is one of the hallmarks of a free society. Consequently, regulation of these members of the law profession by the State must, so far as by human ingenuity it can be so designed, be free from State interference, in the political sense, with the delivery of services to the individual citizens in the State, particularly in fields of public and criminal law. The public interest in a free society knows no area more sensitive than the independence, impartiality and availability to the general public of the members of the bar and through those members, legal advice and services generally.*[2]

3. Although, as suggested by the Supreme Court of Canada in the case quoted in paragraph 2 of this commentary, the independence of the bar may be of particular importance in the fields of public and criminal law, it is important in every area of practice that the client is confident that all advice and representation provided by the lawyer is not influenced by any government ties. The legal profession has a unique position in the community. Its distinguishing feature is that it alone among the professions is concerned with protecting the person, property, and rights of citizens from whatever quarter they may be threatened and pre-eminently against the threat of encroachment by the State. It is the responsibility of lawyers to protect clients' rights, and in order that they may continue to do so there can be no compromise in the principle of freedom of the profession from interference, let alone control, by government.

---

[1] ABA-MC Canon 5, EC 5-1; Alta. 9-R.3; Que. 3.06.05.
[2] *Canada (Attorney General) v. Law Society (British Columbia)*, [1982] 2 S.C.R. 307.

APPENDIX - PRINCIPLES OF CIVILITY
FOR ADVOCATES

PREAMBLE

Civility amongst those entrusted with the administration of justice is central to its effectiveness and to the public's confidence in that system. Civility ensures matters before the Court are resolved in an orderly way and helps preserve the role of Counsel in the justice system as an honourable one.

Litigation, however, whether before a Court or tribunal is not a "tea party". Counsel are bound to vigorously advance their client's case, fairly and honourably. Accordingly, Counsel's role is openly and necessarily partisan and nothing which follows is intended to undermine those principles. But Counsel can disagree, even vigorously, without being disagreeable. Whether among Counsel or before the Courts, antagonistic or acrimonious behaviour is not conducive to effective advocacy. Rather, civility is the hallmark of our best Counsel.

Although couched in terms of proceedings before the Courts, the principles which follow are, with necessary adjustments, applicable to all forms of dispute resolution proceedings, including administrative bodies, arbitrators and mediators. These principles are not intended as a code of professional conduct subject to enforcement by discipline or other sanction but as an educational tool for the encouragement and maintenance of civility in our justice system.

PART I - RELATIONS WITH OPPOSING COUNSEL

General Guidelines for Relations with Opposing Counsel

1.   Counsel should always be courteous and civil to Counsel engaged on the other side of the lawsuit or dispute. It is the

responsibility of Counsel to require those under their supervision to conduct themselves with courtesy and civility as well.

2.   Ill feelings that may exist between clients, particularly during litigation, should not influence Counsel in their conduct and demeanour toward opposing Counsel.

3.   Counsel should always be honest and truthful with opposing Counsel.

4.   Counsel should conduct themselves similarly towards lay persons lawfully representing themselves or others.

Cooperating with Opposing Counsel

5.   Counsel should avoid unnecessary motion practice or other judicial intervention by negotiating and agreeing with opposing Counsel whenever practicable.

6.   When Counsel is about to send written or electronic communication, or take a fresh step in a proceeding which may reasonably be unexpected, Counsel ought to provide opposing Counsel with some advance notice where to do so does not compromise a client's interests.

Communications with Opposing Counsel

7.   Counsel should respond promptly to correspondence and communications, including electronic communications, from opposing Counsel.

Promises, Agreements, Undertakings and Trust Conditions Given to Opposing Counsel

8.   Counsel should fulfill or comply with all promises to, or

agreements with, opposing Counsel, whether oral or in writing.

9. Counsel should not give any undertaking that, to Counsel's knowledge or belief, cannot be fulfilled and should fulfill every undertaking given. Undertakings should be confirmed in writing and should be unambiguous in their terms. Undertakings should also be fulfilled as promptly as circumstances permit.

10. If Counsel giving an undertaking does not intend to accept personal responsibility, this should be stated clearly in the undertaking itself. In the absence of such a statement, the person to whom the undertaking is given is entitled to expect that Counsel will honour it personally.

Cooperating with Opposing Counsel on Scheduling Matters

11. Counsel should consult opposing Counsel regarding scheduling matters in a genuine effort to avoid conflicts.

12. In doing so, Counsel should attempt to accommodate the calendar conflicts of opposing Counsel previously scheduled in good faith for hearings, examinations, meetings, conferences, vacations, seminars or other functions.

13. Counsel should agree to reasonable requests for scheduling changes, such as extensions of time, provided the client's legitimate interests will not be materially and adversely affected.

14. Counsel should not attach unfair or extraneous conditions to extensions of time. However, Counsel is entitled to impose conditions appropriate to preserve rights that an extension might otherwise jeopardize. Counsel may also request reciprocal scheduling concessions but should not unreasonably

insist on them.

15. Counsel should promptly notify opposing Counsel when hearings, examinations, meetings or conferences are to be cancelled or postponed.

Agreement on Draft Orders

16. When a draft order is to be prepared to reflect a Court ruling, Counsel should draft an order that accurately and completely reflects the Court's ruling. Counsel should promptly prepare and submit a proposed order to opposing Counsel and attempt to reconcile any differences before the draft order is presented to the Court.

Conduct Which Undermines Cooperation Among Counsel

17. Counsel should avoid sharp practice. Counsel should not take advantage of, or act without fair warning to opposing Counsel, upon slips, irregularities, mistakes or inadvertence.

18. Counsel should not falsely hold out the possibility of settlement as a means of adjourning a discovery or delaying a trial.

19. Subject to the Rules of Practice, Counsel should not cause any default or dismissal to be entered without first notifying opposing Counsel, assuming the identity of opposing Counsel is known.

20. Counsel should not record conversations with opposing Counsel without consent of all persons involved in the conversation.

Conduct at Examinations for Discovery

21. Counsel, during examination for discovery, should at all times conduct themselves as if a Judge were present. This includes avoiding inappropriate objections to questions, discourteous exchanges among Counsel and excessive interruptions to the examination process.

22. Counsel should not ask repetitive or argumentative questions or engage in making excessive or inappropriate self-serving statements during examination for discovery.

23. The witness who is being examined should be treated with appropriate respect and should not be exposed to discourteous comments by opposing Counsel or their clients.

24. Counsel should instruct their witnesses as to the appropriate conduct on examination and the requirement for courtesy and civility to opposing Counsel and their clients.

25. Counsel should not engage in examinations for discovery that are not necessary to elicit facts or preserve testimony but rather have as their purpose the imposition of a financial burden on the opposite party.

Comments Made About Opposing Counsel

26. Counsel should avoid ill-considered or uninformed criticism of the competence, conduct, advice, appearance or charges of other Counsel. However, Counsel should be prepared, when requested, to advise and represent a client in a complaint involving other Counsel.

27. Counsel should not attribute bad motives or improper conduct to opposing Counsel, except when relevant to the issues of the case and well-founded. If such improper conduct

amounts to a violation of applicable disciplinary rules, however, Counsel should report such conduct to the appropriate professional disciplinary authority.

28. Counsel should avoid disparaging personal remarks or acrimony toward opposing Counsel.

29. Counsel should not ascribe a position to opposing Counsel that he or she has not taken, or otherwise seek to create an unjustified inference based on opposing Counsel's statements or conduct.

Accommodating Requests from Opposing Counsel

30. Counsel, and not the client, has the sole discretion to determine the accommodations to be granted to opposing Counsel in all matters not directly affecting the merits of the cause or prejudicing the client's rights. This includes, but is not limited to, reasonable requests for extensions of time, adjournments, and admissions of facts. Counsel should not accede to the client's demands that he or she act in a discourteous or uncooperative manner toward opposing Counsel.

31. Counsel should abstain from obstructing any examination or court process.

32. Subject to applicable practice rules, Counsel should give opposing Counsel, on reasonable request, an opportunity in advance to inspect all evidence or all non-impeaching evidence.

PART II - COMMUNICATIONS WITH OTHERS

Communications with Other Parties and Witnesses

33. Counsel should not communicate upon, attempt to negotiate or compromise a matter directly with any party who is represented by Counsel except through or with the consent of that Counsel.

34. Counsel may tell any witness that he or she does not have any duty to submit to an interview or to answer questions posed by opposing Counsel, unless required to do so by judicial or legal practice.

Communications with the Judiciary Outside of Court

35. As a general principle, unless specifically provided in the Rules of Practice, a Practice Direction or a Notice to the Profession, Counsel should not communicate directly with a Judge out of Court about a pending case, unless invited or instructed to do so by the Court.

36. Counsel should not contact a Judge in regard to administrative matters, unless otherwise invited or instructed by the Judge. Requests to schedule urgent matters should be made through the court office to the scheduling co-ordinator or an administrative Judge. Other matters such as management, scheduling etc. should be arranged through the Judge's secretary.

37. Prior to a hearing, when dealing with process and procedure, Counsel who wish to communicate with a Judge should do so through the Judge's secretary and advise whether opposing Counsel has been notified and whether consent to the communication has been obtained. The Judge will then determine the appropriate manner of receiving the

communication and advise Counsel.

38. Counsel should not contact a presiding Judge about the case during the course of a hearing unless invited to do so.

39. Unless invited or permitted by the judiciary, correspondence, e-mail or voicemail between Counsel should not be copied to the Court.

40. Telephone conferences that include a Judge are Court proceedings and, while less formal, are subject to the same principles of civility as any other Court proceeding.

PART III - TRIAL CONDUCT

Trial Preparation

41. Counsel should not attempt to handle a trial or matter that he or she is not by experience or training competent to do. Nor should Counsel attempt to handle a trial or matter without preparation appropriate to the circumstances.

42. Counsel should cooperate with other Counsel in the timely preparation of a trial brief of documents to facilitate the management of documentary evidence at trial by the Court, witnesses and Counsel.

43. Counsel should cooperate in the timely exchange with opposing Counsel of any required witness lists and witness 'will-say' statements.

44. If adjournment is sought, Counsel should provide as much notice as possible to the Court and other Counsel, together with the reason the adjournment is requested.

45. Counsel should avoid hostile and intemperate communication among Counsel at all times, particularly close

to trial when stress levels are high. Such communication will only deteriorate further during the trial and adversely affect the administration of justice in the case.

During Trial

46. Counsel should introduce themselves to the court staff at the opening of trial, if not already known to them. The court staff should be treated with appropriate courtesy and respect at all times.

47. During trial, Counsel should not allude to any fact or matter which is not relevant or with respect to which no admissible evidence will be advanced.

48. Counsel should not engage in acrimonious exchanges with opposing Counsel or otherwise engage in undignified or discourteous conduct that is degrading to their profession and to the Court.

49. During trial, Counsel should not make any accusation of impropriety against opposing Counsel unless such accusation is well-founded and without first giving reasonable notice so that opposing Counsel has an adequate opportunity to respond.

50. Objections, requests and observations during trial should always be addressed to the Court, not to other Counsel.

51. Objections during trial are properly made as follows:

(1) Counsel rises and calmly states "Your Honour, I have an objection";

(2) When Counsel rises to make an objection or to address

the Judge, other Counsel should be seated until the Judge asks for a response. Under no circumstances should two or more Counsel be addressing the Court at the same time;

(3) The basis for the objection should be briefly and clearly stated. Following a clear statement of the objection, Counsel should present argument in support of it and then sit down;

(4) Counsel opposing the objection shall in turn, or as directed by the Judge, rise and clearly state their position. They will then make their argument, if any, in support and sit down; and

(5) Usually, Counsel who made the objection will then be given an opportunity to reply. The reply should address only those points raised by opposing Counsel and avoid repetitious re-argument of the issues.

52. When the Court has made a ruling on a matter, Counsel should in no way attempt to re-argue the point or attempt to circumvent the effect of the ruling by other means.

53. In the absence of a jury, a question to a witness by Counsel should not be interrupted before the question is completed for the purposes of objection or otherwise, unless the question is patently inappropriate.

54. Counsel should never attempt to get before the Court evidence which is improper. If Counsel intends to lead evidence about which there may be some question of admissibility, then Counsel should alert opposing Counsel and the Court of that intention.

55. When addressed by the Judge in the courtroom, Counsel

should rise. When one Counsel is speaking the other(s) should sit down until called upon. Counsel should never remain with his or her back turned when the Judge is speaking.

56. Counsel cannot condone the use of perjured evidence and, if Counsel becomes aware of perjury at any time, they must immediately seek the client's consent to bring it to the attention of the Court. Failing that, the Counsel must withdraw. Nothing is more antithetical to the role of Counsel than to advance the client's case before the Court, directly or indirectly, on the basis of perjured evidence.

57. Counsel, or any member of their firm, should not give evidence relating to any contentious issue in a trial.

58. In trials where they are acting as Counsel, Counsel should not take part in any demonstrations or experiments in which their own person is involved except to illustrate what has already been admitted in evidence.

59. Counsel should be considerate of time constraints which they have agreed to or which have been imposed by the Court.

60. Counsel should not communicate with a Judge following a hearing and during deliberation unless specifically invited or directed to do so. A request for consideration of additional factual or legal material should be brought by motion on notice to opposing Counsel.

Any additional legal authority may occasionally be brought to the attention of the Judge and opposing Counsel at the same time but without further comment by Counsel.

If there is a request to make further submissions, the Judge will determine whether further submissions are justified.

61. If you are successful in the case, shake the hand of your opponent if it is offered. Offer yours if it is not. If you lose the case, don't whine. However painful, offer your hand to your successful opponent. If the case is reserved and you have lost, call your opponent with your compliments.

PART IV - COUNSEL'S RELATIONS WITH THE JUDICIARY

What Judges Can Expect from Counsel

62. Judges are entitled to expect Counsel will treat the Court with candour, fairness and courtesy.

63. Judges are entitled to expect that Counsel appearing are by training and experience competent to handle the matter before the Court.

64. Notwithstanding that the parties are engaged in an adversarial process, Judges are entitled to expect that Counsel will assist the Court in doing justice to the case.

65. Judges are entitled to expect Counsel to assist in maintaining the dignity and decorum of the court room and their profession and avoid disorder and disruption.

66. Judges are entitled to expect Counsel to be punctual, appropriately attired and adequately prepared in all matters before the Courts.

67. Judges may expect Counsel to properly instruct their clients as to behaviour in the court room, and any court related proceedings. Counsel are expected to take what steps are necessary to dissuade clients and witnesses from causing disorder or disruption in the court room.

68. Judges are entitled to expect that Counsel, in their public statements, will not engage in personal attacks on the judiciary or unfairly criticize judicial decisions.

What Counsel Are Entitled to Expect of the Judiciary

69. Counsel are entitled to expect Judges to treat everyone before the courts with appropriate courtesy.

70. Counsel are entitled to expect that Judges understand that while settlement is always desirable, there are some cases that require judicial resolution, and that in balancing interests, neither Counsel nor the parties should be unduly urged to settle in such cases.

71. Counsel are entitled to expect Judges to maintain firm control of Court proceedings and ensure that they are conducted in an orderly, efficient and civil manner by Counsel and others engaged in the process.

72. Counsel are entitled to expect that Judges will not engage in unjustified reprimands of Counsel, insulting and improper remarks about litigants and witnesses, statements evidencing pre-judgment and intemperate and impatient behaviour.

73. Counsel are entitled to expect Judges, to the extent consistent with the efficient conduct of litigation and other demands on the Court, to be considerate of the schedules of Counsel, parties and witnesses when scheduling hearings, meetings or conferences.

74. Counsel are entitled to expect Judges to be punctual in convening all trials, hearings, meetings and conferences. If Judges are delayed, they should notify Counsel when possible.

75. Counsel are entitled to expect Judges to endeavour to

perform all judicial duties, including the delivery of reserved judgments, with reasonable promptness.

76. Counsel are entitled to expect Judges to use their best efforts to ensure that court personnel under their direction act civilly towards Counsel, parties and witnesses.

ABBREVIATIONS

Short-form reference to Codes of Conduct are as follows:

Alta   *Code of Professional Conduct* of the Law Society of
            Alberta, November 2002. The Code is divided
            into Statement of Principle (S.O.P.), Rules, and
            Commentary.

ABA-MC   *Model Code of Professional Responsibility* of the
            American Bar Association (Chicago), adopted
            with effect from January 1, 1970, last amended in
            August 1980. The ABA-MC is divided into
            Canons, Ethical Considerations (ECs) and
            Disciplinary Rules (DRs).

ABA-MR   *Model Rules of Professional Conduct* of the American
            Bar Association, adopted August 2, 1983, last
            amended in 2003.

B.C.   *Professional Conduct Handbook* of the Law Society
            of British Columbia (Vancouver), last amended
            May 11, 2004.

N.B.   *Code of Professional Conduct* of the Law Society of
            New Brunswick, adopted with effect from
            January 1, 2004.

N.S.   *Legal Ethics and Professional Conduct Handbook* of
            the Nova Scotia Barristers' Society (Halifax),
            1990.

Ont.   *Rules of Professional Conduct* of the Law Society of
            Upper Canada (Toronto), adopted with effect
            from November 1, 2000, last amended June 28,
            2002.

Que.   *Code of Ethics of Advocates*, R.R.Q., 1981, c. B-1,
            r.1, under *An Act Respecting the Barreau du Québec*.
            R.S.Q., c. B-1 and the *Professional Code*, R.S.Q., c.
            C-26.

BIBLIOGRAPHY

The following is a selected bibliography of texts and other sources helpful to those concerned with matters addressed in this Code:

Bennion, F.A.R., Professional Ethics, *The Consultation Professions and Their Code* (London: Chas. Knight, 1969).

Casey, James T., *The Regulation of Professions in Canada* (Toronto: Carswell/Thomson, 1994).

Goulet, Mario, *Le droit disciplinaire des corporations professionnelles* (Cowansville, Québec, Éditions Yvons Blais, 1993).

Hazard, Geoffrey C. *Legal Ethics: A Comparative Study* (Stanford: Stanford University Press, 2004).

Hutchinson, Allan C., *Legal Ethics and Professional Responsibility* (Toronto: Irwin Law, 1999).

Lundy, Derek, Gavin MacKenzie & Mary V. Newbury, *Barristers & Solicitors in Practice* (Markham, Ontario: Butterworths, 1998).

MacKenzie, Gavin, *Lawyers and Ethics: Professional Responsibility and Discipline*, 3d ed. (Toronto: Carswell/Thomson, 2001).

Orkin, M.M., *Legal Ethics: A Study of Professional Conduct* (Toronto: Cartwright & Jane, 1957).

Perell, Paul, *Conflicts of Interest in the Legal Profession* (Markham, Ontario: Butterworths, 1995).

Poirier, Sylvie, *La discipline professionnelle au Québec, principes législatifs, jurisprudentiels et aspects pratiques* (Cowansville, Québec, Éditions Yvon Blais, 1998).

Proulx, Michel & David Layton, *Ethics and Canadian Criminal Law* (Toronto: Irwin Law, 2001).

Service de la formation permanenet, Barreau du Québec, *Développements récents en déontologie, droit professionnel et disciplinaire* (Cowansville, Québec, Éditions Yvon Blais, publication annuelle).

Smith, Beverly G., *Professional Conduct for Lawyers and Judges* (Fredericton, N.B.: Maritime Law Book, 1998).

Wolfram, Charles, *Modern Legal Ethics* (St. Paul, Minn.: West, 1986).

INDEX